The *Joy* of Recognition

Designing and Implementing
A Successful Recognition Program

Lynnette Younggren and Debra Sikanas

Acknowledgments
Let's Get Started

Index of topics and contributors

Key to Graphic Icons

 Anecdotes from recognition practitioners are marked with this icon.

 These icons represent three different styles of program implementation encompassing different budgets, manpower and commitment levels.

Acknowledgments

Thank you, Baudville folks...

Joe Naimo, for making the text come alive with your wonderful interior and cover design.

Stelle Slootmaker, for your creative insight, editing and proofreading.

Diane Newton, for your research and interviewing contributors.

Thank you, Liz Milo, Kathe Farris, Janis Allen and Susan Galloway for your editing suggestions.

Thank you Roger Bean and Russell Radford, for your encouragement and support.

Thank you Cherri Westhouse and Susan Younggren, for your fun, but practical, ideas.

Foreword

What's more fun than food?

These authors remind us that recognition, like food, is the fuel for life.

Using this book, you will cook up a FEAST of recognition for your co-workers. Debra and Lynnette have doubled their recipes for appetizing, positive aromas to permeate the workplace.

I like the versatility of this cookbook. Reading it can be an elegant dinner with many courses, enjoyed in one sitting. It can also be a plate of bite-sized morsels for grazing during a second read. They're like good leftovers – sometimes even tastier the second time around.

These authors had the courage to tell us about recipes that failed, and had to be stuffed down the disposal. This just gives us the confidence to try ourselves.

I read *The Joy of Recognition* from soup to nuts in an hour and 20 minutes. But I'll go back and snack on individual chapters when I need an energy boost.

Whatever you do, read chapter 12 right now. Once you taste it, you'll want to serve it to your co-workers while it's hot.

Janis Allen
author of *I Saw What You Did and I Know Who You Are*

Let's Get Started...

We all want to be seen; we all want to make a difference. We all want our work to be meaningful. Recognition can make these three aspirations a reality. The Joy of Recognition gives you recipes and ingredients for recognizing the positives in each other.

In one African tribe, people greet each other with the words "I see you." This greeting acknowledges and honors a person. It grants recognition.

Recognition – the manner in which we say "I see you" – comes in many forms. It can be formal and structured, like a black tie banquet. It can be casual, like a snack or picnic. Recognition can be initiated by an organization. Awards and incentives usually fall in this category. Just as important, casual "day-to-day" recognition can be given by a whole spectrum of people – peers, supervisors, managers, suppliers and customers.

"WE ALL NOTICE VALUABLE BEHAVIORS BY OUR CO-WORKERS. RECOGNITION IS MAKING YOUR NOTICE NOTICED."

JANIS ALLEN

Our focus is on such day-to-day recognition – recognition is much more powerful when it happens all the time, for the little things. Like food and water, recognition feeds a basic need. We can survive for some time without any or just a little, but we have more energy when we get it every day.

Different people need different amounts of food to feel satisfied. By the same token, we each enjoy different kinds of feedback and encouragement. Nonetheless, the basic need remains.

The Joy of Recognition will show you how to acknowledge effort, superior performance and a job well done. It will expound the importance of sincere thank yous and encouraging words. And, it will show you how to show appreciation with words, small tokens, non-monetary rewards and awards.

We have given you practical, ready-to-use ideas that you can implement, no matter what size company you have. This veritable cookbook of recipes and techniques serves as an essential handbook for managers and team members alike. Use it yourself, or as a basis for recognition training.

Program recipes and examples from companies who use recognition are woven in throughout the book. Read through them. Try the ones that sound good. Modify them to suit your situation.

We want you to have a tool for establishing recognition-giving as a positive habit, bringing new energy and enthusiasm to your organization. You, your organization and all the individuals you work with will profit when you recognize the positives in people's performance. Enjoy your feast!

Do write in this book. Make notes on every recipe you try. Write the date tried, the results and notes on modifications made to the recipe or modifications you would try next time.

Goals put in writing are much more likely to be met. Let's get started...

What do you want to accomplish by using this book?

For Yourself:

_____

_____

_____

_____

_____

For Your Organization:

_____

_____

_____

_____

_____

☐ A culture where people want to do their best

☐ A fun, energetic environment

☐ A systematic way to approach recognition

☐ Buy-in for more recognition programs/efforts

☐ An organization that attracts new staff

☐ Improved individual attitudes

☐ Organizational profitability and growth

☐ Improved employee satisfaction scores

☐ Reduced absenteeism and turnover

Recognition
Fuel For Business Results

CHAPTER 1

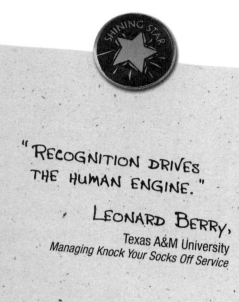

Gas engines, plants and humans all need "fuel," an energy source. Recognition fuels the human spirit and psyche just as food and water fuel the physical body. True, humans have different energy needs. Some need more than others. Some can stay alive on less, but thrive when given more. In the plant world, some plants will only send out blossoms if they receive enough energy. Humans are the same. Wouldn't you rather have a "blossoming" company of thriving, energetic people than a crop of drooping leaves?

"RECOGNITION DRIVES THE HUMAN ENGINE."

LEONARD BERRY,
Texas A&M University
Managing Knock Your Socks Off Service

Feedback – recognition of positive performance – can be that energy source. Systems designers build in feedback loops so companies can get frequent feedback. Take this away and the company would suffer. Successful businesses track measurable indicators – profit and loss, sales, etc., in order to operate efficiently and effectively. They watch these indicators closely, day by day, week by week, month by month.

People also want to know, "How am I doing?" They need this feedback daily, weekly, monthly… if they don't get it, how can they turn good performance into habitually good performance? How can they make improvements to meet expectations? Take feedback away and both the individual and the company suffer.

Recognition:

- Is positive reinforcement. When we have a positive consequence for our behavior, we're more likely to repeat it.
- Reinforces behaviors that are important for organizations to be successful.
- Confirms achievement.
- Helps people choose to excel.
- Reinforces commitment.

Simply put: you get what you reward. We're suggesting that the reward be recognition.

OK, now that we've agreed that everyone hungers for recognition, let's take an inventory of who those people are in your life. Yes, people who work for us need our recognition. But don't stop there. Can you think of others who deserve recognition for deeds they've done for you or for accomplishments they've achieved? Your boss may be the most overlooked person on the list. Bosses are people, too. And don't forget your co-workers. They all need "recognition food" for fuel!

Make It Personal

Write down names in each category. We will refer to this page later.

People who work for you	People you work for	People you work with	Suppliers internal /external	Customers internal/external	Outside of work

Additional Considerations

Looking back over the past six to twelve months, what major workplace milestones came and went without acknowledgment?

_____

_____

_____

Could your organization have benefited from more recognition? How?

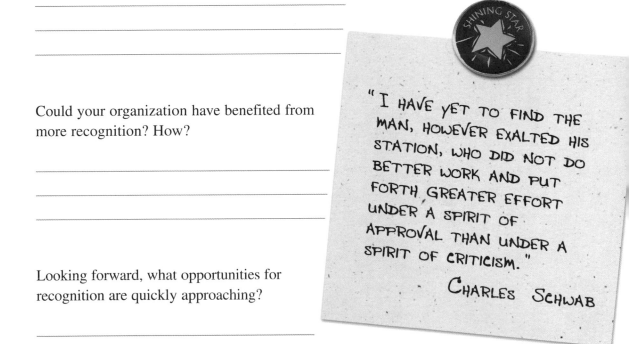

_____

_____

_____

"I HAVE YET TO FIND THE MAN, HOWEVER EXALTED HIS STATION, WHO DID NOT DO BETTER WORK AND PUT FORTH GREATER EFFORT UNDER A SPIRIT OF APPROVAL THAN UNDER A SPIRIT OF CRITICISM."

- CHARLES SCHWAB

Looking forward, what opportunities for recognition are quickly approaching?

_____

_____

_____

How will your organization celebrate them and collectively learn from all that happens? Start thinking and planning.

_____

_____

_____

What goals have you or your company set for your group?

_____

_____

_____

How is positive reinforcement provided along the way?

_____

_____

_____

What are some of the obstacles you and others face in providing timely, meaningful recognition to one another? What steps can you take to overcome these obstacles? How can you help others overcome them, too?

Obstacle	How To Overcome	How To Help Others

Look back at your list of people to recognize on page 1.4. How have they made a difference? As the next two weeks unfold, keep a list of the people you are going to recognize, acknowledge, thank and appreciate.
Then DO IT!

Name _____ *should be recognized for:*

_____

_____

_____

Name _____ *should be recognized for:*

_____

_____

_____

Name _____ *should be recognized for:*

_____

_____

_____

Name _____ *should be recognized for:*

_____

_____

_____

Name _____ *should be recognized for:*

_____

_____

_____

The Key Ingredient

Making The Case For Recognition

Participants at the Eighth NAER (National Association for Employee Recognition) Recognition Sharing Conference in May 1999 were asked, "What is the greatest challenge that you face as an employee recognition professional?" More than 40% said, "Management buy-in, management support, involvement at all levels." This response has resounded in every workshop NAER has held.

> "THERE IS GREAT VALUE IN RAISING THE LEVEL OF ASSOCIATE (EMPLOYEE) SATISFACTION. WE'VE SHOWN THAT BY INCREASING ASSOCIATE SATISFACTION, CUSTOMER SATISFACTION GOES UP AS WELL. IT IS NO COINCIDENCE THAT OUR TOP FIVE STORES IN PERFORMANCE ARE ALSO THE STORES THAT SURVEYS HAVE SHOWN RECEIVE THE HIGHEST RECOGNITION SATISFACTION SCORES."
>
> FRED HIBBEN
> *Manager of Associate Recognition for Sears*

Your greatest challenge as an employee recognition professional will be to sell the importance of recognition to your organization's leadership. Then, you'll need to sell it to people at all other levels in order to maximize involvement.

Q. Why do I need to get management buy-in and support?

A. Two reasons: one, if leadership believes recognition is valuable, then levels throughout the organization will follow because they are often rewarded for doing so. Two, most likely, management will have to approve the budget and use of time for recognition programs.

Q. How do I make the case for employee recognition programs to management?

A. In order to sell anything, you have to know your customer and what they want. Let them know what's in it for them. A company is in business to make money. Make the picture clear. Your mission is to show how a recognition program can help the company make or save money. It's about the bottom line.

Liz Milo, founder of Motivationery and former recognition manager for AT&T says, "Recognition could be likened to an extension of the company recruitment process, designed to retain the quality work force that your company has worked to build. And, the potential for a reduction in turn-over has positive impact to the company's bottom line, so a financial case can be made that links recognition to profitability and a positive ROI. One can also build a case for recognition as a building block for customer retention. This strategy again underscores recognition as a positive for the financial bottom line, as opposed to simply a generous 'people process.'"

Your Well-Constructed, Strategically Linked Recognition Program:

- Translates company values into specific work habits.
- Focuses efforts on achieving specific goals.
- Tells people what is really important to the organization.
- Helps deploy goals and create links to strategic business initiatives.
- Meets people's needs for recognition of achievement and efforts.
- Creates an energetic, fun environment.

This Recognition Program Can Result In:

- An engaged work-force who understands how actions, behaviors and attributes affect business success.
- Profitability and growth.
- A culture where people want to do their best.
- An organization that attracts new staff.
- Improved individual attitudes.

- Reduced absenteeism and turnover.

- Successful teamwork.

Next, as you design and implement your program, a survey can measure the current climate on the recognition issue. This survey will provide a quantitative basis for your case for recognition and establish the baseline for evaluating progress after you've implemented your program. Results gathered in this post-implementation survey, compared to the pre-implementation survey, can demonstrate your program's performance and suggest improvements for the future.

Q. Why does recognizing people for their efforts and results promote behaviors that help achieve company goals?

A. Reinforcement theory explains why. We're not talking about some dust covered, boring postulates. We all actually use it in many ways in our daily lives.

Prompted by the research of renowned behavioral psychologist B. F. Skinner (1904-1990), reinforcement theory emphasizes the importance of feedback and rewards in motivating behavior. Recognition and knowledge of results are forms of feedback. Basically, the theory states that people will repeat behavior with favorable consequences, while people will not repeat behavior with unfavorable consequences. In other words, you get what you reward. The theory describes four types of consequences for behaviors.

Theory One: Positive Reinforcement

We get something we want. You work extra hours on a project and your boss takes you out to lunch to thank you. Or, you help a co-worker on a project and he writes you a thank you note. This positive reinforcement can be in the form of praise, encouragement, recognition, promotions or tangible rewards.

Theory Two: Negative Reinforcement

We avoid something we don't want. In order to avoid a low rating on your performance review, you arrive at work every day on time.

Theory Three: Punishment

We get something we don't want. We are yelled at because we came back late from lunch.

Theory Four: Extinction

We don't get what we want. The behavior goes away. For example, we clean the kitchen at work every day, even though it isn't part of our job description. We secretly hope and expect to receive praise from our co-workers. We don't receive praise, no one comments, so we stop doing it. Silence (no feedback), although unintentional, can cause someone to stop doing something.

Positive reinforcement in the form of praise, encouragement and recognition is a powerful tool for shaping behavior. By defining the behaviors that accomplish company goals, recognizing those behaviors and rewarding them, you will increase the likelihood that those behaviors will recur. Over time, the three stages of this cycle build positive habits.

Stage One
Make the desired behaviors known.

Stage Two
Notice the behaviors when they occur.

Stage Three
Praise the person performing the behavior as soon
after the behavior as possible.

Dr. Aubrey C. Daniels has written an excellent resource on the link
between behavior and consequences: "Bringing Out The Best In People:
How to Apply the Astonishing Power of Positive Reinforcement."
During his presentation at a recent NAER Recognition Sharing Conference,
Daniels said, "positive reinforcement, to be effective must be: valued,
contingent on individual performance, immediate and frequent."

Daniels notes, "Most managers feel that doing nothing has no effect on
performance. But doing nothing is doing something to performance."[1]

Providing no feedback can have undesirable consequences that managers
must be aware of (extinction). It's quite the opposite of giving recognition.
It's ignoring! It's silence. No news is good news? Consider this scenario.
You volunteer to help your boss by staying late for no extra pay and do not
receive a "thank you." Will you feel your help was valued? Will you feel
appreciated? Will you volunteer again? Probably not.

By explaining this basic human need for praise to management, you will have
more success in gaining their support. Stay tuned for more tools and tangible
evidence of recognition's value to the organization in the following chapters.
We'll help you enlist "buy in" from management and staff on all levels.

[1]Dr. Aubrey C Daniels <u>Bringing Out The Best In People</u>. New York: McGraw Hill, Inc., 1994
Reproduced with permission of McGraw Hill Companies.

Menu Planning Basics

Determining The Scope Of The Program

CHAPTER 3

When planning an event for guests, you decide how many people to invite, who to invite, and how elaborate or elegant you want the event to be. How do you decide? You look at your own skills as a cook and hostess, your budget and how much effort you want to invest.

Solo Flyer

In planning your recognition program, you need to decide who will participate and how elaborate it will be. Will it be a program for your team? For your department? Or for your entire company? Will it be simple or complex? What is your budget, your manpower and your commitment? In other words, are you Flying Solo? Do you have a Task Force? Or, are you leading a Corporate Initiative?

Task Force

These three different styles of recognition program implementation encompass different budgets, manpower and commitment levels. Preparing a feast with 20 different dishes wouldn't be practical for one cook serving a four person party. By the same token, if you're Flying Solo, running a recognition program with 20 different options won't be practical for you. Deciding who you are can define your course of action. It can help you decide whether you will act on your own, present your ideas to your boss or make a presentation and proposal to top management. You may start Flying Solo and end up leading a Task Force or heading a Corporate Initiative, depending on your results.

Corporate Initiative

Any size company can use any of these approaches. Base your choice on:

Budget

How much money do you have to spend? A sizable fiscal budget, a generous one-time commitment or what happens to be left over in petty cash?

Manpower

Are you the only one who has realized the power of recognition? Do you have a small team who is ready to cook up a recognition meal with you? Or has top management committed to a recognition culture?

Commitment

How many people are committed to using recognition on a regular basis in your company? Just you? A group of trend-setting managers? Or, a separate, funded department?

Solo Flyer

Flying Solo

You're Flying Solo if…

Budget: You have no budget for recognition.*

Manpower: You're the only one who is willing to spend time giving recognition.

Commitment: No one else really cares.

The good news… Flying Solo can accomplish a lot of good with a little planning and less money. Your quick-start recognition program could be compared to stopping at the deli for a few snacks. And, you don't need to convince anyone before you get started.

One person can make a difference. Watch "It's A Wonderful Life" if you need further convincing. In this movie, Jimmy Stewart discovers, through experience, how the way he has lived his life has had a positive impact on people around him. He has made a positive difference.

*See Chapter 7 for low cost ideas.

Take-Off – Getting Started:

Goals: what results are you looking for? You're Flying Solo now, but are you going to try to enlist the help of a co-worker or two? Gandhi began alone and look how he ended up!

_____

_____

_____

Roles:

You're it! Read the rest of the book and complete all the assignments that apply to your situation. Of course, you have all the action items on YOUR list.

Plans:

How do you achieve the result you want? First, identify existing behaviors that will help achieve your result. Then, start recognizing people accomplishing those behaviors with praise or a thank you when they use them. For example, you're the manager of customer service and you want to improve customer satisfaction in your call center. You have identified one way to get this result: manage customer expectation by giving them a time and date when you will get back to them with an answer to their question. When you hear customer service representatives giving callers this information, you stop by their desks and compliment them.

Often we don't get tasks done until we write down what actions we're going to take and assign a deadline to each action. Filling in the blanks on the following page will confirm your commitment to your recognition project. Think of the nutritious food you will be serving and the energy that will come from it.

If this exercise seems difficult to fill out now, finish reading the book and come back to it later.

Recognize who?	For what behavior?	What will you do?
_____	_____	_____
_____	_____	_____
_____	_____	_____

Up-Selling

Gaining support or approval from people in higher authority can help you make a better success of your recognition program. You are the best judge of your company, but we suggest sharing your plans with your boss, at least. Invite top management to participate in one of your activities, for example, giving a token of appreciation or recognition. This will put an official stamp of approval on your plans while opening the door for your program to spread and grow.

Task Force

The Task Force

A Task Force requires:

Budget: you have a small budget to use for recognition.

Manpower: a small number of people want to start a recognition initiative.

Commitment: those people are willing to commit time to the process.

You're small in number, but remember that an apple tree grows from one tiny seed and produces bushels of nutritious apples. In other words, if you each bring a dish to pass, you could have a memorable meal.

Commence Operation Recognition

Goals: What results will put your organization on target? What do you want to accomplish?

_____

_____

_____

Roles:

Who's going to do what? Fill in the plan below so everyone knows their assignments.

If this section seems difficult to fill out now, finish reading the book and come back to it later.

Who?	Will do what?	To achieve this result
_____	_____	_____
_____	_____	_____
_____	_____	_____

Budget:

How much money do you have to spend on supplies?

Plans:

Often we don't get tasks done until we write down what actions we're going to take and assign a deadline to each intention. Scheduling is a commitment. Don't forget to write your actions in your planner. Enjoy your potluck!

Recognize who?	For what behavior?	What will you do?

Corporate Initiative

Corporate Initiatives

Your Corporate Initiative will require:

Budget: $15 - $30 per employee

Manpower: Many people, including some who have been giving recognition as part or all of their job description.

Commitment: The organization's goal is to get everyone committed from the top down.

With this vision of a positive, value driven culture, plan on preparing a banquet fit for a king. You have the power behind you and the whole company is cheering you on. Top executives <u>must</u> have the same vision for the recognition program as the program designers (strategic alignment).

When you're going for a corporate-wide initiative, implementation may be more labor intensive than you had expected. Break it down into manageable steps. That way, you will solve the three biggest challenges recognition specialists face:

1. Management buy-in

2. Management support

3. Involvement from all levels

Whether you have to sell "up" to get buy-in, support and budget allocations or sell "down" and "across" to get involvement, remember: people take action when something is in it for them. Your mission is to figure out what that something is and give it to them. Another key to buy-in is ownership, getting people to feel like they helped create the recognition program. Be sure you include people from all levels in planning and implementation. Keep bosses and top management involved by letting them present the awards or tokens of appreciation. This will also add importance to the occasion for the recipient.

Are you Flying Solo or working with a Task Force? Turn to Chapter 6 to learn how to design your initiative. Are you leading a Corporate Initiative? Proceed to the next chapter and be prepared to lead a group discussion at your next lunch meeting.

Planning The Menu

Goals, Roles And Plans

CHAPTER 4

Planning The Menu: Goals, Roles and Plans

Aligning your recognition program with the company vision, mission, values and operating philosophy will help you make your case. Measuring key performance and employee satisfaction indicators will give you evidence of its results. Carefully designing, communicating, training, implementing, tracking and tweaking your program will raise the participation level and quality of your program. Keep in mind, you are planning a very large celebration banquet. You can't simply pull out a recipe, shop for ingredients the night before and prepare it the day of the celebration. Careful thought and planning as well as following several recipes step by step, will ensure your feast is memorable and spectacular. Even more important, plan when you will take each step and how long each step will take to complete. When we first began hosting dinner parties, we did not bother with planning out our timing. Our guests often waited until 10:00 p.m. to eat. Don't let your guests wait around hungry! Your program may lose impact and support.

If you are the program's initiator, plan your presentation to upper management carefully. Know your audience. This flow chart will help you plan the process.

Determine the Strategic Link
▼
Measure
▼
Ask
▼
Design
▼
Communicate/Invite
▼
Train
▼
Implement
▼
Track/Measure
▼
Tweak

4.3

Determine the Strategic Link

Who	Content	Format	When
Initiator(s)	Why are we setting up a recognition program?	Written	Week 1
Initiator(s)	What do we want to accomplish?	Written	
Upper Management, Design Team	How does it support our company mission, vision, values and guiding principles?	Facilitated group discussion; written	Week 2
Upper Management, Design Team	Create a recognition program mission statement.	Facilitated group discussion; written	Week 2
Initiator(s), Upper Management, Design Team	How are we going to measure the program's impact? What are the indicators? Turnover? Absenteeism? Customer Satisfaction? Employee Satisfaction? Quality? Safety?	Facilitated group discussion; written	Week 2
Per Company Budgeting Process	How much money will be budgeted for the program?		Week 3
Design Team	Who will be the upper management program champion?	Facilitated group discussion; written	Week 3
Design Team	Who will play which roles in the project?	Facilitated group discussion; written	Week 3

This approach has many benefits. When your recognition program is strategically linked to company goals, it can show the entire organization the connection between the goal and the actions of each individual. In other words, this approach makes it easier for each individual to see how he or she can contribute to the goal.

This approach also gives clarity to you, the program champion. You, and the others working with you, will gain confidence and direction as you communicate and move through each design and implementation phase. The time you invest now will be paid back many times over. This approach also increases the program's value for top management, so you'll gain the support you need for success.

An automobile manufacturer made the strategic link. They recognized and praised staff behaviors that helped the company achieve its mission. Each quarter, people nominated people they worked with (up, down and across) for excellent work in any one of several categories. The supervisor and manager signed the nomination. The nominees received an award certificate at an awards ceremony attended by supervisors, managers and senior management; the plant supervisor gave out the awards.

"The best rewards and recognition programs are linked to goals that are, in turn, linked to better business."

Gillian Flynn
Workforce, July '98

Freedom Village in Bradenton, Florida, links their recognition program to recruitment and retention. They have set up programs which make Freedom Village a desirable place to work. The unemployment rate is very low in their area so recruiting and retaining employees is a high priority.

Another company uses recognition to reinforce the behaviors which exemplify employee empowerment – taking care of the customer without going through layers of staff. This links to the company vision of "uncompromised customer service." Recognizing people who go out of their way to solve problems for the customer encourages them to repeat the positive behavior.

Jean Hand at Super Vision International, a manufacturer of fiber optics in Orlando, Florida, says, "What we're trying to accomplish is taking care of the customer and we realize to do that we have to take care of the employees as well. That's the first step. If your employees aren't happy, your customers won't be either." In this way, they have linked recognition with their strategy.

Recognition Program Mission Statement

Writing mission statements may not be your forte, so here are some samples. Even great cooks don't make everything from scratch.

 Kathe Farris, Recognition Professional at BankBoston, shares this recognition statement: "We reinforce the behaviors that directly attribute to our corporate values of initiative, integrity, diversity, and teamwork."

 Liz Milo described the mission of AT&T's P.R.I.S.M. (Partner Respect Innovation Service and Merit) Team as: "To fully support the achievement of our Vision, Mission and Values statements through providing the tools for positive reinforcement among our Partners."

 Fred Hibben, Sears Manager of Associate Recognition, says: "The objective at Sears is to recognize associates, creating a win-win scenario. The associate (employee), feeling appreciated, is happier in his/her day-to-day activities which translates into superior performance and customer service; a win for the associate and for the company."

 Debbie Patrick, formerly of AT&T Universal Card, had her own recognition mission statement: "To seize every opportunity to recognize the efforts and accomplishments of others."

Determining Your Strategic Link

Why are we setting up a recognition program?
Example: To reinforce the use of our new values.

_____

_____

What do we want to accomplish?
Example: People "live" the values as seen in their day to day behaviors.

_____

_____

How does it support our company mission, vision, values and guiding principles?
Example: Our company vision is to provide exemplary customer service. Our values exemplify behaviors which support that.

_____

_____

Using this data, create a recognition program mission statement.
Example: To quickly seize every opportunity to recognize a person who is "living" one or more of our values.

_____

_____

How are we going to measure impact of program? What are your indicators?
Example: Customer satisfaction, customer retention.

_____

_____

How much money will be budgeted for the program?
Example: $15.00 per person for materials (not labor).

_____

_____

Who from upper management will champion the program?

Example: The President of the organization.

_____

_____

Who will play which roles in the project?

Example: Human Resource Manager will lead and oversee the program. Managers and Team Leaders will communicate concepts and information while recognizing people for their positive behaviors. Client Relations will design and distribute the customer satisfaction survey. Accounting will compute and produce reports and graphs for the customer satisfaction and customer retention surveys.

_____

_____

Measure

Who	Content	Format	When
Design Team	Determine who will be gathering and reporting measurements decided upon in stage 1.		Week 3
	Design an employee survey for baseline recognition satisfaction feedback.		Week 3
	Create a baseline of other indicators.		Week 4
	Administer employee recognition survey.		Week 5
	Create a report of baseline data on employee recognition satisfaction.		Week 6

Determine "Who" and "Format" based on the scope of your individual recognition initiative.

Your pre-implementation baseline will prove critical later when you compare it with post-implementation numbers. If you're tempted to save this step for later – don't. Make your choices, get commitments from the people who will collect the data and those who will present it in an easily readable format. Follow up with these people on a regularly scheduled basis to be sure you're collecting the figures that correctly measure your results.

Appropriate measurements could include absenteeism, turnover, customer satisfaction, customer retention, profit, employee satisfaction or quality.

Kathe Farris revealed, "for the first time, in 1995, BankBoston conducted an employee satisfaction survey that was the reason for starting an employee recognition program."

Stand alone survey statements for your larger climate baseline employee satisfaction survey.

☐ I receive timely and meaningful recognition when I exceed expectations or go above and beyond in my work (use past six months as benchmark reference).

☐ I receive frequent feedback about how I am doing in my job.

☐ I feel appreciated for the work I do.

☐ I am satisfied with the amount of recognition I receive for my efforts.

☐ I receive recognition for my efforts at work from the person I report to.

☐ I receive recognition for my efforts at work from co-workers.

☐ I give recognition for his/her efforts to the person I report to.

☐ I give recognition for his/her efforts to my co-workers.

☐ I tend to perform better when I understand how my work contributes to the company and feel that my efforts are appreciated.

Liz Milo says, "This (recognition measurement) became a short two to three question section on our division's climate survey. Using that tool, we were able to create statistically valid links between the use of recognition and overall satisfaction of employees, which reduces costly employee turnover. With that data, we were also able to tie employee satisfaction with overall satisfaction of clients. Results from a 1993 employee survey lead to the allocation of people and resources to address gaps in employee satisfaction and respect issues. Once the programs were designed and deployed, recognition-specific questions were added to the annual climate survey to determine program strengths and opportunities for improvement. Linking all the data together from both internal and client surveys helped forge a statistical link between use of the program and employee satisfaction, and between employee satisfaction and client satisfaction/retention."

Menu Preferences
Input From Guests

CHAPTER 5

Menu Preferences: Input From Guests

*H*ave you ever had guests over for dinner who ate very little of their food and declined the wine completely? It sure puts a damper on the evening's gusto – especially when the main event was that elaborate meal you spent hours preparing. We know. It has happened to us. We prepared a five course French meal, with appropriate wines chosen to match each course. We didn't know the guests well, except in a business setting. It didn't occur to us to ask about their eating and drinking preferences in advance. Their preference for low-fat foods and abstinence from alcohol totally clashed with our high-fat, French dishes and their accompanying vintages. The result: we all felt awkward and disappointed.

The message here – get input from your guests on their tastes and preferences. For your recognition program this means – ask for input from the people who will be using the program before you design it. This will give you two benefits. One, the ideas and opinions you gather will help you make better design choices. Two, and of equal importance, you will foster buy-in which comes from involvement. Remember, we love what we create.

Ask

Who	Content	Format	When
	Input from employees on what motivators are.	Focus groups, email, surveys	Week 6
	Brainstorm ideas for low-cost recognition.	Focus groups, email, surveys	Week 6

Determine "Who" based on the scope of your individual recognition initiative.

How you handle this stage depends a great deal on your organization. Some may eliminate it and only use input gathered from the employee recognition satisfaction survey.

Example questions for an employee focus group:

- What motivates you to put effort into your job?
- What small tokens of appreciation for a job well-done would you enjoy?
- What would you like to be recognized for?
- How would you like team recognition to be done?
- What if one or two people on the team do most of the work?

To make this process easier, use the *Tell Us About You!* survey card provided in Chapter 18.

Example questions for an employee survey:

- What small tokens of appreciation for a job well done would you enjoy?

Suggest items you're thinking of using in your program. And, always solicit these preferences in a manner allowing for anonymity.

- Rate your preference for recognition gestures by giving each item below a number from 0-10 indicating your preference intensity. 0 is no interest, 10 is a very high preference:

    ____ A verbal thank you

    ____ A private, written thank you

    ____ Movie theater tickets

    ____ Public announcement with applause

    ____ Public presentation of an award

    ____ A subscription to a magazine

    ____ A gathering of people with food

    ____ Time off with pay

    ____ Interesting job assignment

    ____ Invitation to become a member of a project team

Even if you don't implement all the responses you collect, be sure to follow up with a thank you. Let the people who took time to give their opinions know that you appreciate their efforts.

Menu Decisions
Program Designs

CHAPTER 6

Solo Flyer

Before you start choosing your recipes, you'll need to answer some essential questions.

Task Force

- Will your program be emanating from you alone (Flying Solo), comprise a small group of people (Task Force) or be company-wide (Corporate Initiative)?

- If it's a company-wide program, will it be broad-based, meaning the same for everyone, or departmental, meaning initiated and designed within specific departments?

Corporate Initiative

  In cooking terms, are you going to cook all the dishes and just have the guests show up? Or, are you going to have a potluck with everyone deciding what to bring individually? Both styles have benefits, but your organization's size will determine which style works best.

- Will departments decide what they will do individually? If so, then give each some guidelines and a budget. Let them decide what they will recognize, what acknowledgments or rewards they will use and how they will award them.

Motorola, in Plantation, Florida, does this. By putting the recognition program at the departmental level, people may feel closer to the goals.

- Will your program be formal and structured or, informal and day-to-day?

Formal recognition programs are the most prevalent and are often what people think of when you first mention "recognition program." These measurement-based programs outline specific guidelines for achievement. However, informal, day-to-day, peer-to-peer recognition can have greater impact because it touches more people, more often. It better reinforces and creates habits of desired behaviors. Also, recognition that does not have a high dollar-value attached minimizes issues of inequity (She's getting more than I am; I've done the same thing; why wasn't I given that reward?) and entitlement (I deserve and expect this; it is a part of my benefits package).

FORMAL

Recognition Given for...
- Length of service
- Anniversaries *(see Chapter 8 for ideas arranged by price category)*
- Attendance
- Safety
- Achievement
- Sales goals

Type...
- Top down

Use...
- Award certificates
- Award trophies
- Plaques
- Creative objects that are meaningful to your company or the individual
- Company logo items

INFORMAL, DAY-TO-DAY, ON-THE-SPOT

Recognition Given for...
- Positive behaviors
- Achievement
- Commendations
- Thank yous

Type...
- Lateral, vertical, interdepartmental

Use...
- Pocket Praise
- Thank you notes
- Post-it notes
- Star goodies bag
- See Chapter 7.3 for ideas arranged by price categories

What is the culture of your company? Creative? Fun? Formal? Top Down? Team Oriented? Structured? Conservative?

Program design should follow the culture of your company. If you are very measurement-oriented, design recognition based on measurement. An old adage says, "If you measure it, people will do it. If you measure it and pay for it, people will do it in spades." We're suggesting you "pay for it" in the currency of recognition as well as more tangible rewards (if that fits your culture).

If you have a fun, creative environment, design your recognition program to live that spirit. Your program can help set the tone for a new strategy. For instance, if your company is conservative, and your strategy is to be more entrepreneurial, you can reinforce behaviors that encourage this.

The following flow chart gives you a structured approach to design.

Susan Galloway, Training Manager with Navigant International, worked through these steps. With many ideas flowing from a number of people, the picture lost form at times. To keep her thoughts clear, and assist others in seeing the big picture, she created a storyboard. She assigned a different color adhesive note paper to each person, or position (e.g. company president, managers, team leaders). She wrote one idea per paper and placed them on a two-by three-foot foamcore board. The notes were placed on the board by order of usage: pre-implementation, kick-off, implementation and post-implementation. As an added benefit, when she wanted to tell people about the plans, she pulled out the board and explained them visually. She reported to me that this helped more people see the big picture much more quickly.

Design

Who	Content	Format	When
Design Team	Translate company vision, values and principles into behaviors. What specific behaviors or activities support each one?	Facilitated group discussion, written	Week 7, 8, 9
Design Team	Sort the behaviors into 3 lists • Those that only require individual effort • Those which require team effort • Those which require organization-wide effort.	Facilitated group discussion, written	Week 7, 8, 9
Design Team	Decide for each behavior whether you want a • Formal-Structured Program • Informal-Day-to-Day • Or Both	Facilitated group discussion; written	Week 7, 8, 9
Design Team	Will the program be broad-based or departmental?	Facilitated group discussion; written	Week 7, 8, 9
Design Team	Objectives for each program	Individual assignment, presented to team; written	Week 7, 8, 9
Design Team	Criteria for giving	Individual assignment, presented to team; written	Week 7, 8, 9
Design Team	Who is the target audience? Who do we want to recognize?	Individual assignment, presented to team; written	Week 7, 8, 9
Design Team	Who is eligible to nominate?	Individual assignment, presented to team; written	Week 7, 8, 9
Design Team	Who is eligible to give?	Individual assignment, presented to team; written	Week 7, 8, 9
Design Team	What is available to give (or the price range).	Facilitated group discussion; written	Week 7, 8, 9
Design Team	Where are items stored and how are they obtained.	Facilitated group discussion; written	Week 7, 8, 9
Design Team	When will it be given?	Individual assignment, presented to team; written	Week 7, 8, 9
Design Team	Where will it be given?	Individual assignment, presented to team; written	Week 7, 8, 9
Design Team	Who is going to model the desired behaviors?	Individual assignment, presented to team; written	Week 7, 8, 9
Design Team	Who is going to administer the details?	Facilitated group discussion; written	Week 7, 8, 9

You may wonder why the flow chart instructs you to sort desired behaviors into two lists (those which can be objectively measured and those which can't). Formal, structured programs work better with objectively measured behaviors. Rules for achievement are clearly defined. For example, when meeting or exceeding sales goals, a person receives an award, trophy or trip. If you are using rewards with a higher dollar value, clearly defined rules for achievement give people a map and reduce perceptions that rewards are presented inequitably.

The flow chart then states, "Sort the behaviors into three lists – those that only require individual effort, those which require team effort, and those which require organization-wide effort." These are listed in descending order of control for the individual. We control our own results the most, team results less and organizational results the least. I will probably be most motivated to achieve goals which I can control most. (In case you're interested in the theory behind this – it's expectancy theory). Emphasize frequent, individual positive reinforcement in your recognition program. Personal, specific, immediate thank yous can truly make an impact. Celebrations and small, memory-value items motivate teams. You should also give private, one-on-one praise to individual team members who make the greatest effort. Celebrations, where we share our feelings of accomplishment, appropriately recognize company-wide achievements.

Both formal and informal programs have their place in your recognition program. By answering the flow chart questions and asking for input from guests, you have better defined the character of the menu. By having your answers in writing, you develop a stable plan that others can refer to. Now for the fun part – cooking up that program. Peruse our recipes and choose the ones that fit your organization's special-order recognition menu.

Design with a Theme In Mind

A theme can be an excellent way to communicate concepts and add fun to the program. It gives people an easy way to remember desired behaviors and creates a rally cry. A theme also makes the the program more memorable.

San Antonio Teachers Credit Union linked their recognition program to their "TEAMWORK 2000" values. San Antonio Teachers Credit Union defined behaviors that would support its vision, created a theme and designed a logo for TEAMWORK 2000.

TEAMWORK stood for Truthfulness, Empowerment, Adaptability, Motivation, Wisdom, Ownership, Respect, Knowledge. The TEAMWORK values evolved out of management brainstorming sessions. These values were displayed on posters in many locations, including publicly so customers could see them. "We will honor at least one person who exemplified Truthfulness, another who exemplified Empowerment, and so on," says Lisa Fairal, of San Antonio Teachers Credit Union.

Recipes
From Budget To Gourmet

CHAPTER 7

Before you choose a recipe, you may want to stock your pantry with basic ingredients. Sometimes neither your budget nor your appetite can handle a fancy, full course gourmet meal. Low-cost snacks fill the need. They're fast, convenient and fun to eat. Other times you want to treat yourself to a full menu of the finest foods available. Do start out with these two basics:

• Software to create award certificates.

• Border paper to print awards on.

Award certificates can be formal or informal. Even cute and fun. Keep several papers on hand – formal, themed, holiday and event-oriented.

MEMORY VALUE

TANGIBLE ITEMS INVITE OPPORTUNITIES TO RE-LIVE THE GOOD FEELING. WHEN WE LOOK AT A WRITTEN NOTE OR OBJECT CONNECTED TO A POSITIVE EVENT, IT CONTINUES TO REINFORCE US. AND WHEN SOMEONE ELSE SEES IT, AND ASKS ABOUT IT, WE CAN RE-TELL THE STORY AND RELIVE THE GLORY!

The Recognition Pantry

Under $5.00

- Your time
- A smile
- A thumbs up
- A post-it note of appreciation
- A stop for an ice cream cone
- Gift certificate for fast food or a video rental
- Decorative pencils
- A thank you note
- Stickers
- Candy
- A soda pop
- A potted perennial from your garden
- Homemade cookies
- A package of gold adhesive stars
- Invitation to join a team project
- Invitation to coach, train or mentor a co-worker
- Job assignment of personal interest
- The words "thank you"
- A day named after them
- Flowers from your garden in a jar
- Badges engraved with years of service
- Pocket Praise – easy to carry and quick to personalize

- Dollar store fun items
- Lapel pins
- Mini size T.E.A.M. Lifesavers and Breathsavers®
- Squeezable Praise stress relief toy
- T.A.G. Team Acknowledgment Guy bean-bag toy
- Chocolate Rewards
- Motivational stickers

Under $10.00

- A motivational calendar
- A mug or tumbler with candy
- Baseball cap
- Award certificate in a frame
- Lapel pins
- Company logo items
- Book
- Flowers
- T.E.A.M. Paper Cube
- Phone card with free minutes
- Golf balls – personalized for your organization
- Car wash coupons

Under $20.00

- Tickets to a movie (for two)
- A computer screen saver
- A magazine subscription
- Tee-shirt
- Picture frame
- T.E.A.M. tote bag
- Travel Mug – personalized for your organization
- Umbrella
- Applause, Applause Celebration Gift Tumbler

Under $30.00

- T.E.A.M. sweatshirt
- Star clock
- Thanks a Million gift box
- Gift certificate for an on-line bookstore or music store

Now, let's get cooking!

Connect Card

Submitted by: Lori Bruins, Performance Improvement Coordinator at Zeeland Community Hospital.

Purpose: To make it easy for peers to recognize each other's good deeds and achievements. To increase the scope of positive behaviors managers "see." To expand the benefit of an act of recognition giving.

Serves: An organization, a department. Informal, day-to-day.

Ingredients: Pre-printed, two-part perforated thank you note. Vehicle for easy access to cards, such as clear plastic holder placed in frequently used locations – for example, near copy machines.

Directions: Advertise the availability of the cards and make it easy for people to know how and when to use them.

• Make the cards easily accessible.

• Encourage peers to use them to acknowledge and praise good deeds and achievements.

• Communicate to managers that they are responsible for asking the recipient why they got the card and give them praise.

File managers copy of card in the employee's personnel file and refer to it during their performance review.

Result: Opportunities for feeling the joy of recognition are multiplied.

Staff at all levels show appreciation.

A World of Thanks

Submitted by: Debbie Patrick, formerly of AT&T Universal Card Services.

Purpose: A powerful peer-to-peer recognition program to encourage a culture of appreciation.

Serves: An organization, a department. Informal, day-to-day.

Ingredients: A round piece of heavy card stock paper imprinted with a watermark of the globe in the background and thank you in many different languages. Retrieval bins in high traffic areas for collecting responses.

Directions: Send all associates 3 to 5 blank cards twice a year.

Communicate that these are to be given to anyone in appreciation of efforts or accomplishments. No approval is needed, no restrictions.

Explain the World of Thanks program in new employee orientation and give them a small supply of blank cards.

Result: One of their most effective programs.

Community Volunteers

Submitted by: Sherri Bradford-Royle, Volunteer Service Manager, Porter Hills Presbyterian Village.

Purpose: To thank volunteers who have given their time.

Serves: Volunteers.

Ingredients: A theme - "wellness" was the 1999 theme. A gift for each volunteer - aromatherapy candles. Speaker - on topic which supports the theme. Border paper for the invitation. Snacks and beverages. Prizes– special tee shirts, monogrammed throw blankets, tote bags, watches with volunteer services logo.

Directions: This event is held each year in April during Volunteer Appreciation Week. All items used in the event are coordinated around the theme for the year. Volunteers and their guests are invited to a social hour followed by a speaker and excellence awards. Sherri does not do a "volunteer of the year" award to emphasize hours of service. She does not want to praise one person at the expense of others. People give the amount of time they can, and each person's time is valued.

Result: A feeling of being valued and camaraderie among volunteers. A committed volunteer staff who continues to share their time.

The Character Award

Submitted by: Debbie Patrick – this recipe was used by one department at AT&T Universal Card Services.

Purpose: To create fun recognition.

Serves: A department. Adds fun.

Ingredients: A set of characters. For six months, they might use Loony Toons characters. For another 6 months, Disney characters.

Directions: The group chooses the person who displays the attributes of the character. For example, give the Tasmanian Devil award to a person who always rushes around to get things done.

Result: Fun and energy.

You Made a Good Point

Submitted by: Lynnette Younggren

Purpose: To encourage and reinforce the generation of ideas.

Serves: Departments, teams.

Ingredients: Logo or special pencils. For example, T.E.A.M. pencils.

Directions: Give everyone five pencils. Tell them to give them to people when they have a good idea.

Results: More ideas.

Picture This

Submitted by: Lynnette Younggren

Purpose: To give new employees a feeling of belonging and connection to their new co-workers.

Serves: An organization.

Ingredients: Snap Together Buttons, photos, special bingo cards.

Directions: Ask new employees to bring a photograph of someone or something important to them on their first day. (Be sure to indicate that the photo will not be returned.) The photo could be of anything — a loved one, a pet, a flower, a sight. Use the Snap Together Button to make a pin-on button with the photo. Give each employee a bingo card.

Ask employees to stop and introduce themselves to people wearing the button. The photo could be a conversation starter. Have the new employee sign the bingo card.

At the end of the day, people who have a bingo get a prize. If you have a lot of people and want to make the prize bigger, have everyone who has a bingo put their cards in a drawing for a prize.

Modification: For a company that doesn't have a number of employees starting on the same day, eliminate the bingo game.

Results: The new employees comes in the second day feeling more comfortable and connected.

Walk 100 Program

Submitted by: Richard W. Austin, Director of Staff Development, Grand Rapids Community College.

Purpose: To encourage healthy behaviors.

Serves: An organization.

Ingredients: A set of goals and rewards for each goal.

Directions: During a two-month period, reward employees for each 25 miles they walk. At 100 miles, award t-shirts and enter them in a drawing for a day off with pay. Adjust milestones to meet your staff's abilities.

Results: A healthy, energized staff.

Teamwork 2000

Submitted by: Lisa Fairal, San Antonio Teacher's Credit Union.

Purpose: To reinforce behaviors which support company values.

Serves: An organization.

Directions: San Antonio Teachers Credit Union linked their recognition program to their *TEAMWORK 2000* values. Lisa Fairal says "We want rewards and praise to be tied to this. TEAMWORK stands for Truthfulness, Empowerment, Adaptability, Motivation, Wisdom, Ownership, Respect, Knowledge. These values are displayed on posters in many locations, including publicly so customers can see them. Every quarter a group of volunteers select a person or people who best exhibited each value. So we will honor at least one person who exemplified Truthfulness, another who exemplified Empowerment, and so on." The TEAMWORK values evolved out of a survey they gave to everyone in the company.

Results: A staff focused on the TEAMWORK 2000 values.

Stars and Stripes

Submitted by: John Griswold of Woodville, New Hampshire.

Purpose: To thank donors and volunteers, the patrons who donated money, and the Fourth of July committee who donated time to organize and bring about the city's Fourth of July parade with 70 floats, six bands, food, rides and fireworks each year.

Serves: Volunteers, non-profits, municipalities.

Ingredients: Stars and Stripes border paper, Award Maker Software.

Directions: Design and print a certificate of appreciation for each volunteer.

Results: People in the city keep sharing their time and money.

Recognize Your Patients

Submitted by: Jill Lindemoen, a dentist office associate and dental association and OMS member.

Purpose: To encourage patients to refer others.

Serves: Organizational sales.

Ingredients: Award Maker software, award paper, seals.

Directions: Print awards for patients who refer a new patient.

Results: Increase in the customer base.

Build Your Club

Submitted by: Jill Lindemoen, OMS, an international professional development organization with 160 local clubs in the United States and Europe.

Purpose: To retain and add members and sustain high attendance at each meeting.

Serves: A club.

Ingredients: Small prizes, Award Maker software, award paper.

Directions: Each month attendees are awarded certificates for attendance and outstanding contributions. These are given ceremoniously in front of the entire group. Door prizes are also given each month.

Results: Jill's club, with 240 staff members and 60 dentists, ranks first among 160 clubs, based on their record of retaining members.

The PYI Suggestion Program

(Provide Your Input)

Submitted by: Lori Bruins, Performance Improvement Coordinator at Zeeland Community Hospital.

Purpose: Process improvement.

Serves: An organization.

Ingredients: Suggestion forms, form holders.

Directions: Place PYI Suggestion forms in various locations. Use clearly visible holders attached to the wall or set on a desk-top. Ask employees to share ideas on how to improve a process by completing the form, signing their name and turning it in. By turning in a PYI form, the employee offers to take part in the solution. Lori sends the forms to the manager most likely to be affected by the change. The manager responds directly to the initiators and includes them in implementing the solution.

Place PYI forms into a quarterly drawing. Zeeland Community Hospital gives $50.00 restaurant gift certificates. The program is promoted in the hospital's internal newsletter.

Results: Many employees working at and improving company processes.

Baudville "Bucks"

Submitted by: Baudville Creative Staff.

Purpose: Promote exceptional customer service performance by gaining familiarity with company products.

Serves: A department.

Ingredients: Blue and gold 3-up certificate paper, Award Maker software, Pocket Praise, jumbo postcard or thank you cards. Blue certificates were valued at $1 and gold ones at $5.

Directions: A new catalog contained many new products. Baudville wanted to expand the opportunity for service people to "own" these new products. For 60 days, award Customer Service Representatives meeting your criteria "Your Company Name" Bucks. The Baudville Bucks were currency for purchasing the new products. For example, Baudville awarded Bucks weekly for perfect attendance, going above and beyond, working through a lunch to cover phones, or volunteering for an errand or project. Present the Bucks with a thank you card or pocket praise stating the reason for recognition.

Results: Increased familiarity with products, raised morale, fun and a more confident staff. Customer Service Representatives feel best about their job when they can speak confidently and enthusiastically about products to customers who ask about them.

Three Cheers

Submitted by: Lori Bruins, Performance Improvement Coordinator at Zeeland Community Hospital.

Purpose: To encourage people to go above and beyond.

Serves: Organizations, top-down, informal recognition.

Ingredients: Movie tickets, video rental gift certificates, gift shop gift certificates.

Directions: When you want to thank an employee or team leader for going above and beyond, give them a Three Cheers token of appreciation: movie tickets, video rental or other gift certificates.

The Connect Card (see recipe) can initiate the idea to give a Three Cheers token of appreciation.

Results: Staff that feels appreciated for their extra efforts.

Helping Hands

Submitted by: Rose Landre, HR, The Gillette Company, Santa Monica, California.

Purpose: To acknowledge the efforts of employees who volunteer.

Serves: Volunteers.

Ingredients: Helping Hands border paper from Baudville and Award Maker software.

Directions: Each person who volunteers their time for projects, such as the American Heart Association and Jimmy Stewart Marathon, receives an award certificate.

Result: Volunteers who feel appreciated.

T.A.G., You're It

Submitted by: Lynnette Younggren

Purpose: To show support and acknowledge effort and achievement.

Serves: Teams.

Ingredients: T.A.G. (A bean bag type figure wearing a tee shirt imprinted with "T.A.G." *Team Acknowledgment Guy*).

Directions: When people on your team have a bad day, hand them T.A.G. and tell them how much they're appreciated. Or, if a team member has something to celebrate, like a big sale, send T.A.G. over with congratulations. You can also make your own rules for passing T.A.G. around.

Results: Team members who feel appreciated.

You're a Star

Submitted by: Eva Parker,
First Nationwide Mortgage.

Purpose: To recognize above and beyond service.

Serves: Peer-to-peer, day-to-day.

Ingredients: Large gold stars and gold star-embossed adhesive seals.

Directions: Have each department determine the criteria for giving recognition. Anyone can give recognition; anyone can be the receiver. The first time a person receives a star that is hung above the recipients cubicle. Subsequent recognition is rewarded with embossed stars placed on a navy blue presentation folder. At the end of the month, stars are totaled and used towards gifts of differing values, based on the number of stars earned.

Results: People who feel appreciated and eager to earn "stars" and the gifts that follow.

Wall of Fame

Submitted by: Eva Parker,
First Nationwide Mortgage.

Purpose: To recognize above and beyond service.

Serves: External customer to staff recognition.

Ingredients: A wall to display letters.

Directions: When a customer sends a letter of appreciation, place it on a Wall of Fame with a star attached.

Results: People who feel proud of their work receive positive reinforcement over and over again.

Only the Best!

Submitted by: Pam Bell, Human Resource Communications/Services Senior Specialist, Meijer, Inc.

Purpose: To sincerely recognize everyone in the company for everyday job performance.

Serves: At Meijer, thousands.

Ingredients: Verbal praise and thank yous, pre-printed thank you notes with a place for the name of the recipient and the giver, small tangible gifts.

Directions: If you see someone doing their job well, say "thank you" and tell them that what they are doing is important. You may also give them an "Only the Best!" note. Red thank yous can be given by anyone in the company. Gold notes (given by director level staff) say "Extra Special Thank You!" and can be given by director level staff. These have an extra tear-off coupon good for a complimentary beverage. Use other colors for special events or seasons.

Each month any recipient of a thank you note can put it in a box used for a drawing. An example of a drawing reward would be a $5 gift certificate for use in a Meijer store. Many gift certificates are given each month. The company surveyed team members and the feedback was that they would prefer more people receive gift certificates rather than a few people receiving high value certificates.

Some people keep the "Only the Best!" notes and display them in their work area rather than put them in the drawing. They say they prefer to have the visual reminder of the "thank you."

Results: People feel appreciated; they know they are important.

You're a Star

Submitted by: Star Service Awards & Recognition Team, Navy Personnel Command, Morale, Welfare & Recreation (MWR) Division (PERS-65).*

Purpose: To recognize outstanding service, accomplishments and special deeds. The guidelines set are "to recognize the customer service behaviors which create a positive, memorable experience."

Serves: Peer-to-peer.

Ingredients: You're A Star mylar balloons, 4-up postcards imprinted with the Star Service logo.

Directions: When you want to recognize someone for providing superior service or for a special accomplishment, surprise them with a "You're A Star" balloon attached to a card detailing the good deed and identifying the giver. Cash incentives, called MWR Bucks that are in the form of $1 gift certificates, are also included. These MWR Bucks can be used at any facility where fees are incurred, such as the fitness facility, the food court, the daycare center, etc.

Results: People who feel like the have made a difference. They are stepping out of their comfort zone. An admiral was so impressed with the results, he is in the process of applying the program to his area. .

*The You're A Star Balloon and Recognition Card and the information above is not necessarily the official view of or endorsed by the US Government, the Department of Defense or the Department of the Navy.

Values in Performance

Submitted by: Darliene Townsend, PNC Bank, Pittsburgh, Pennsylvania.

Purpose: To say thank you to employees who exhibit company values in their day-to-day functions.

Serves: Employee satisfaction and organizational goals.

Ingredients: Company values, thank you cards, certificates, value badges, redemption coupons, gift checks.

Directions: Recognize the behaviors you want to reappear. This can be done peer-to-peer, bottom up, or top down. When you see someone "living" a particular value, such as "Customer Focus," give them a thank you card describing the positive behavior. Enclose a "badge" for that particular behavior (in this case Customer Focus). Each person has a blank certificate on which to place "value badges" as they earn them. When you have earned a total of 10 value badges, turn in your certificate and receive a $25 gift certificate.

Results: People who understand and "live" the values of the company.

The Triple A Award

Submitted by: Stelle Slootmaker, Parent Booster, Horizons Community High School, Wyoming, Michigan.

Purpose: To recognize students who excel at academics, attendance and attitude.

Ingredients: Teachers and a small budget for lunch in a restaurant.

Serves: Schools.

Directions: Teachers nominate students. Parent Boosters read and approve genuine nominations. Award winners receive an award certificate and go out to lunch with the teacher who nominated them.

Results: Students observe that academics, attendance and attitude are valuable behaviors. Relationship building between students and teachers.

The Extra Mile Award

Submitted by: Stelle Slootmaker, Parent Booster, Horizons Community High School, Wyoming, Michigan.

Purpose: To show appreciation for a wide range of commendable behaviors that may be missed by traditional school recognition initiatives.

Serves: Schools.

Ingredients: Nomination Form, Award Maker, Award Paper, Movie Passes.

Directions: Students, teachers, or parents can nominate a student by using a special form available in the school lobby. Once a month the Parent Boosters review the nominations and reward all sincere nominees a certificate and two movie passes. A parent presents the awards during Community Meeting, a weekly get-together attended by all students and teachers. Examples of actions which have won awards are: a group of students who faithfully visited a fellow student in the hospital who had been injured in a car crash; students who helped diffuse a fight in the school yard; students who helped a new lunch lady get used to her job; a student who finished all his semester work in spite of missing two months of school due to an injury.

Results: Builds student self-esteem and shows good ethical behaviors are as important as academics.

Dennis Andrade Day

Submitted by: Debbie Bennett and Heidi Evans, Labor Relations Specialists, CalPERS (California Public Employees' Retirement System).

Purpose: To acknowledge the "above and beyond" efforts of a special person who puts heart and soul into a project. and to celebrate the spectacular results.

Serves: A special individual.

Ingredients: Creativity, teamwork, choose a date.

Directions: Chose a day to devote to one special person. Conjure up personalized, fun activities to show someone how they are appreciated. Here is what CalPERS did. Make your own modifications to fit your audience.

Each of the 8 functional units in HR signed up for an hour time slot to give Dennis special attention. Each unit created a very personalized "thank you" for Dennis and what he had done for that unit. One unit gave him a huge river rock they had all signed. This fits the theme of "the rock" that CalPERS uses in their day-to-day recognition program.

Knowing Dennis is an avid fisherman, one unit made him a basket of fish-shaped cookies. Another, an edible fish-bowl with blue Jello water, gummy fish, candy pebbles in the bottom, a peppermint stick fishing pole, gummy worms for bait, shaved chocolate for sand. Another unit presented a trophy and sang their own words to "Let's Hear it for the Boy."

Result: Fun, camaraderie, and sincere heart-felt recognition. "This was the most fun I've ever had at work" said Tom Petty, division chief. "The giving brought people together. We had a lot on our plate and had lost track of having fun. This event made people feel like they had permission to take time out for recognition and fun. It sparked other divisions to have fun with recognition. We're starting to see more and more examples of people getting creative and having fun with recognition."

You're Framed or I See You

Submitted by: Lynnette Younggren

Purpose: To welcome new employees or members of a team.

Serves: Organizations, teams.

Ingredients: Camera, paper photo frames.

Directions: Each time a new team is formed or a new employee joins the staff, take their picture and put it in a paper frame on the wall.

Results: Pride, feeling of belonging.

HELP

Health Enrichment Lifelong Program

Submitted by: Richard W. Austin, Director of Staff Development, Grand Rapids Community College.

Purpose: To increase health awareness; to recognize and experience how a combination of consistent moderate exercise/activity and healthy lifestyle choices are key to a healthy mind and body.

Serves: An organization.

Directions: Any one in the organization can choose to participate. Each person tracks his/her healthy behaviors and points earned on a log. Designate four levels of achievement. Each level has a different selection of rewards.

Points are earned in four categories. For example, one point is awarded for any of the following choices made during a single day:

Nutrition – eat a morning meal, 2-3 servings of fruits; Exercise/Activity – 15 minutes of continuous activity; Mental Health/Quiet Time – six to eight hours of sleep per night; 15 minutes of dedicated quiet time.

Other Healthy Choices – no tobacco products, wear your seatbelt.

Enter winners in a monthly drawing for pairs of movie passes.

Results: Healthy habits and a healthy workforce.

We're a TEAM

Submitted by: Linda Grassia, Marketing, Langer Biomechanics Group, Inc.

Purpose: To celebrate a new team formed from two different departments.

Serves: Companies that are reorganizing

Ingredients: Ribbon, scissors, TEAM mugs, TEAM pencils and TEAM Lifesavers.

Directions: When two departments were combined to form the Customer Care Area, we had a ribbon cutting ceremony. Everyone received a TEAM mug, and TEAM Lifesavers.

Results: A new TEAM atmosphere.

Please share your recognition recipes. We may just start a recipe exchange club!

www.baudville.com

Recipes
Anniversary Celebrations

CHAPTER 8

Why Celebrate Employee Anniversaries?

Employee service anniversaries are important opportunities for a company to recognize and celebrate the tenure and contributions of individual employees. Such a recognition opportunity, when managed well, can enhance the morale of the work force by underscoring the value the company holds for its people. The same opportunity lost or mismanaged, however, can lead to an erosion in employee morale that can ultimately impact the corporate culture. The company that holds high standards for employee performance, but fails to celebrate employee tenure, sends a loud message proclaiming a corporate double-standard. Additionally, with the cost of employee turnover at an all-time high, celebrating service anniversaries appropriately may help stem the tide of emigrating employees. That makes this recognition program one of the most cost-effective to implement and maintain.

When to Celebrate

Recognize anniversaries annually at one yearly celebration or on service anniversary dates. Make a bigger to-do on benchmark dates, for example, every five years. Some companies celebrate employee tenure in hourly increments of time! You may choose to celebrate one or all of the above. Base your decision on more than budget – company needs can drive your program design, as well. For example, if your organization incurs significant employee turnover costs, consider recognizing tenure more frequently, every six months or even monthly. Celebrating employee service over shorter intervals of time may simply involve a correspondence from the company's leadership or the employee's supervisor. Include mementos for anniversaries celebrating one year or more.

Ask employees what benchmarks they would like to celebrate through surveys or a series of focus groups. Be prepared to canvass all levels of employees, in every location and throughout every shift. Surveys can be short (two to three questions, with an additional space for comments). As an added incentive, award small raffle prizes to those who return their surveys. Share your findings with your company's leadership and also with employees.

How Much to Budget?

Administrative costs aside, you can set program costs by assessing a memento value based on tenure. For example, a large communications company budgets mementos based on the "rule of eight" – service anniversaries are celebrated every five years and mementos are budgeted at $8 per year. A five-year service anniversary memento is valued at $40.00, ten years, $80.00, etc. Using a set dollar amount per year and information provided from human resources files will enable you to effectively create a budget plan for your anniversary program.

Be aware, high spending does not always translate into high value – the manner in which the recognition is shared is often the most important part of the process.

An appropriate service anniversary celebration incorporates the interests of many parties: the employees, their supervisor, and the company's leadership. Consider the employee's personality, likes and dislikes. After all, the most expensive and carefully planned celebration and presentation of a company memento can be meaningless if you ignore the celebrant's preferences.

Supervisors are an important part of the celebration because they are ultimately responsible for the celebration's success. They will know best how to integrate the employee's likes and dislikes into the recognition process. By tagging a high-level message onto the presentation, the company's leadership can under-score linkages between the employee's contributions and the company's goals

and direction. The employee who feels appropriately rewarded for years of service will more likely continue to contribute to the company.

Process Overview

- **Employee tracking and notification.** Depending on the company size, you can track employee service anniversaries via the human resources department or supervisory managers. This process should create a tickler file that prepares for the anniversary in the months preceding the actual date. Tracking system sophistication can be impacted by the number of employees. In small offices, notes on a calendar may suffice. In larger companies, gather information from employee data kept on the human resources database. By linking the process to human resources, you provide an additional quality check for anniversary data.

- **Preparation.** As the service anniversary date draws near, notify the employee's supervisory manager. He or she should manage the celebration. The celebration may include drafting a congratulatory note or formal letter, creating a certificate and planning a presentation that suits the recipient's tastes. If celebrants select their anniversary memento, forward the selection sheet to the employee along with a brief note of congratulations. Additionally, the tickler file can generate a letter from company leadership. This letter should praise the celebrant and create a linkage to company goals and business objectives.

- **The memento.** The memento functions like a business card – it helps create a perception about the firm and acts as an effective advertising tool within both the internal and external labor pool. If your work-force doesn't have existing, traditional memento favorites, you may want to create a list of gifts for the employee to choose from. Preferably, these items would contain the company name and logo as well as the employee's name or monogram. The supervisory manager presents the mementos which have been selected prior to the celebration.

- **Presentation and celebration.** These two key responsibilities belong to the supervisory manager. The celebration can become an agenda item for the next team meeting, a special luncheon or a simple stop at the employee's desk. The celebration's tone is set by the employee – its effective interpretation must be made by the supervisory manager. During the celebration, the employee may be presented with a memento, which should always be accompanied by a letter or note of congratulations that can be copied to their personnel file. Make direct reference to the employee's distinct contributions. You should be rewarding those contributions, not simply noting years on the payroll.

 ## As an aside...

Sometimes we can learn from others' experiences… This story came from one of our contributors.

Though our company was a subsidiary of a large multinational company, we were created during the divestiture and thrived on being "different" from the stodgy and lumbering parent company. Therefore, we did everything our way and followed few corporate sanctions. This included our service anniversary recognition process.

The recognition program was managed by human resources, and worked wonderfully when the company was small, in one location, and when almost everyone knew almost every one else. Our company continued to grow, but unfortunately the process did not. It was being run out of a storage closet, and was absurdly over budget. Charges of favoritism erupted due in part to the lack of standards around memento values. Something had to change, and finding and fixing the something was my responsibility.

In an effort to heal the bleeding budget, I took measures (as I came to recite in many apologies) that placed the value of money over the value of people.

A poor choice. A very poor choice. I decided to use a low-cost catalog company that allowed recipients to select from a number of gifts. The problem was that the gifts were tacky, their quality poor, customer service spotty at best, and the perception by the employees was that something special had been taken away from them. Luckily, the offended were vocal, and I realized very quickly that I had erred. The fix for us was exploring our corporate options, and "linking into" a wonderful service anniversary program supported by a recognized vendor.

Corporate HR shared employee data with the vendor, who in turn notified the supervisory manager in advance of the employee's upcoming benchmark service anniversary. Employees also received an advance mailing that contained a letter from the chairman, a certificate, and a catalog containing lovely premium items, all of which carried (some rather discreetly) the company logo. The service anniversary gift catalogs were printed specifically for our company, and all the administrative costs and shipping costs were included. The budget was approximately $8 per recognized year. ($40.00 for five, $80.00 for ten years, etc.) Employees selected their memento, which was then shipped directly to the supervisory manager for presentation. I provided suggested guidelines for presentations. One of the additional benefits was that the vendor facilitated our budgeting process for the upcoming year by projecting the number of benchmark anniversaries for the following calendar year. Phew. Fixed, and just in time to avoid a mutiny! It was amazing to me the ease with which this program worked… I heard only compliments about the process from that point forward!!!

Memento Suggestions...

LOWER-COST

- Personal letter from the president or senior leadership
- Share of stock (now you work for the toughest boss... you!)
- Award certificate
- Low-cost gift certificate
- Logo embellished desk equipment
- Engraved pen
- Inspirational print
- Business cards
- Business card holder
- Plant (let's grow together)
- Engraved key ring
- Company golf shirt or tee-shirt
- Logo embellished mug with candy
- Calendar (plan your continued success!)
- Lunch with a leader, manager or senior manager
- Service anniversary lapel pin

MODERATELY-PRICED

- Engraved clock
- Embossed leather memo pad
- Day-timers calendar system
- Larger inspirational print
- Lunch with a bigger leader, higher level employee or participation in a focus group held by a company officer
- Logo embellished watch
- Product or service that the company provides
- Participation in career enhancing seminar
- Professional membership
- Service anniversary lapel pin with a gemstone

HIGHER-PRICED

- Golf clubs
- Jewelry
- Service anniversary lapel pin with a diamond
- Crystal
- Dinner with the leadership – employee's family members included
- Sporting equipment

Memorable Service Anniversary Fare

THE FIRST DAY

Day 1

Start their future in the company on a high note with your version of a welcome wagon.

Corporate logo products:

- Mugs, tote bag, etc.
- Apparel
- Pens, Pads, etc.
- Welcome card or memo

THE EARLY YEARS

1 - 10 years

Tokens of appreciation and simple forms of thanks:

- Anniversary card
- Personal interest or hobby book
- Pizza party
- Make-your-own sundae party
- Breakfast celebration
- Casual day in employee's honor (don't forget memo to announce it and name tags to celebrate it)
- Day off
- Share of stock (framing this certificate with a message thanking them for their investment)
- Gift certificate to favorite lunch place
- Press release in local newspaper or association publication

THE ODD-YEARS OUT

In-between years

Some fun and thoughtful things to do...

- Car detailing (perfect when traveling is part of doing business).

- Maid service
- Spa day
- Day off
- Professional or personal interest magazine subscription
- Professional association membership
- Feature or mention in company newsletter
- Name plate displaying years of service
- Scrap book/portfolio of professional accomplishments

MILESTONE DATES
20, 25, 30, 35, 40, 45, 50

Gifts of honor or donation in their name:

- Donation to employee's charity, or cause of their choice
- Donation to Alma Mater
- Volunteer project to the charity or cause of their choice
- Name a section of facility or building in their honor
  (conference room, hallway, etc…)
- Plant a tree in their name
- Name a star in their name
- Include a letter or plaque from company's executive as
  a sentimental keepsake to mark the occasion

LOW COST & FUN IDEAS

When the thought is more than your budget:

- Customized "company greeting card" that celebrates
  employment anniversaries
- Bottle of vitamins – with a note of "thanks for the energy"
- Preserve employee's original ID (bronzed, Lucite, etc…)
- "This is your WORK life" home video directed, produced
  and delivered by colleagues
- Wine or champagne with customized label (personalized
  with employee history and accomplishments)
- Movie or video gift certificate celebrating their Oscar potential

Seasonings

Recipes For Special Seasons And Company Events

CHAPTER 9

Creating recognition events around special seasons and company events can add focus and meaning. It can also add fun. Get a group of people together to brainstorm – you'll be amazed at all the creative ideas you'll come up with.

These recipes are listed by calendar date, starting in January.

A Letter from the President

Submitted by: Liz Milo, Motivationery.

Season: President's Day.

Serves: An organization.

Ingredients: A letter written by the president of the organization.

Directions: Ask your organization's president to write a letter thanking employees for something specific. Suggest he or she mention organizational results and recognize how the contribution of all was important.

I Have A Dream

Submitted by: Lynnette Younggren

Season: Martin Luther King's birthday.

Serves: An organization.

Ingredients: Paper, pencil.

Directions: Invite each person to write down one of their dreams – work or personal. Display them on a wall.

Modification: Have focus groups where people talk about their dreams for the organization. Ask "what would you like our firm to look like or be like in the future?"

Rainbow's End

Submitted by: Baudville Creative Staff.

Season: Martin Luther King's birthday.

Serves: An organization.

Ingredients: Decorations depicting rainbows ending in goals, paper cut-outs of pots of gold, photos of staff emphasizing diversity. The rainbow collage could also be transferred to letter size posters to hand out to each employee.

Directions: Celebrate diversity by creating a bulletin board (or web page) with a rainbow and photos. Give each employee a pot of gold cut-out. Have each write a goal that can be met better through diversity on the pot of gold. Post the pots of gold at the end of the rainbow. If no bulletin board area exists, print individual, letter-sized posters employees can post in their work area.

You're the Heart of Our Organization

Submitted by: Baudville Creative Staff.

Season: Valentine's Day.

Serves: An organization, a department.

Ingredients: Valentines.

Directions: Give each employee a valentine, expressing appreciation for a specific positive he or she brings to the company. Invite employees to post their valentines in the lunch room at the cost of $1 to $5 and donate proceeds to the American Heart Association or other charitable organization.

Valentines for Easter Seals

Submitted by: Liz Milo, Motivationery.

Season: Valentines Day.

Serves: Your community.

Ingredients: Carnations by the stem, small boxes of candy, cupcakes individually wrapped and a dash of creativity and fun!

Directions: This holiday jumble is a great way to support the Easter Seals or other charitable organization within your community. Sell the carnations, candy, cupcakes and flowers as Valentine gifts. Co-workers will appreciate the convenience and the proceeds will help Easter Seals. Make sure you advertise where the proceeds will be going (then you can goad your customers by asking them to "have a heart.") Position your selling tables near doorways so you get a lot of traffic at end of day when Cupids remember they need to bring something home to their better halves!

We're Lucky to Have You Here

Submitted by: Baudville Creative Staff.

Season: St. Patrick's Day.

Serves: An organization, department or classroom.

Ingredients: Shamrock decorations, small prizes.

Directions: Create a bulletin board, web page or small poster depicting a four leaf clover. Write a behavior the company values on each leaf (e.g., punctuality, sales performance, customer service, safety, innovation, perseverance, dependability). Present employees demonstrating those traits with a small token – pen, candy bar, dollar bill – wrapped with a green ribbon.

Take Your Child to Work Day

Submitted by: Liz Milo, Motivationery.

Season: Take Your Daughter/Son to Work Day (April).

Serves: An organization.

Ingredients: Volunteers, snacks, activity tools, a plan.

Directions: Plan a full slate of activities to keep kids busy and teach them about "the real world." Hold workshops on goal setting (create an over-arching goal, and then create smaller steps to reach it). Tour computer areas, mailing facilities. Serve treats in the cafeteria. Have kids create their own business cards (markers, glitter and imagination required). Company leaders share how to overcome challenges to success. Liz says, "(Our) public schools require children who attend these events to write an essay explaining what they saw and learned. I believe our kids have a lot to report."

The Bunny Trail

Submitted by: Baudville Creative Staff.

Season: Easter.

Serves: An organization, department or classroom.

Ingredients: Colored eggs, TEAM Lifesavers, Seeds of Praise.

Directions: Have managers don bunny ears and "hop" from desk to desk, leaving a plastic egg filled with TEAM lifesavers and signed Seeds of Praise cards. Also, encourage the bunnies to offer each employee a personalized, verbal compliment or appreciation pertaining to their job performance.

Cinco de Mayo

Submitted by: Lynnette Younggren

Season: The 5th of May, Mexico's Independence Day.

Serves: Organizational diversity.

Ingredients: Invitations, flags, a film or video, Thank You Post-It notes.

Directions: Invite employees to contribute to a potluck lunch. Suggest Mexican foods or foods from their own ethnic background. Fly a Spanish or Mexican Flag. Show a Spanish or Mexican travel-ogue film or adventure movie in the lunch room. Hand out Baudville Thank You Post-It notes and encourage employees to jot a quick "gracias" telling department co-workers what they appreciate about them.

Mother's Day

Submitted by: Lynnette Younggren

Season: May.

Serves: An organization or department.

Ingredients: Photographs of each person as a baby or child or a photo of a pet. Fun, inexpensive prizes. How about things related to babies or pets?

Directions: Put the photographs on a board and have a contest to see who can match the most pictures with the names of the adults who work in the company. Give out fun prizes.

Mother's Day "Your Plate is Full"

Submitted by: Baudville Creative Staff.

Season: May.

Serves: Working moms within an organization or department.

Ingredients: Paper plates, Baudville Reward Coupons, Baudville Kids Motivational Stickers, chocolate "Hugs."

Directions: Write a note of appreciation on a paper plate, "You do such a great job even though your plate is full!" Have department employees sign it. Staple on a Reward Coupon and a sheet of stickers for the kids. Set each mom's desk for morning coffee, with the plate, a cup of coffee and a chocolate.

Father's Day

Submitted by: Lynnette Younggren

Season: June.

Serves: An organization or department.

Ingredients: Photographs and fun, inexpensive prizes.

Directions: Ask men to bring in pictures of their children to put on a board. Or, if they prefer, a photo of something that represents something important to them, like a restored car, a fishing rod and fish or some other hobby. Have a contest to see who can match the most pictures with the name of the adult who works in the company. Give out fun prizes.

Recognition Kickoff

Submitted by: Debbie Brigham, Director of Quality, Glenayre.

Season: October, National Quality Month.

Serves: A whole organization.

Ingredients: Prizes, Baudville Instant Print Tickets/Write Your Own Ticket— a two-part, perforated ticket with several decorative designs. It works great for raffles, door prizes and more.

Directions: Create the ticket text and feed the Instant Print Ticket through a laser printer. In this case the heading on each ticket said "Thank-Q" (Q for Quality). When you see someone going above and beyond, write their name on the name stub of the ticket and describe what they are being recognized for. Then, put the other section of the ticket, with the employee's name into the suggestion box.

At the end of the month, stubs are pulled from the suggestion box and prizes are awarded. The prize is a coffee mug with the Quality theme on it and personalized with the company logo. The grand prize is a leather bag.

Quality Detective

Submitted by: Liz Milo, Motivationery.

Season: October,
National Quality Month.

Serves: A whole organization.

Ingredients: A trench coat and fedora hat.

Directions: The leadership team masquerades around in a trench coat and fedora, prowling around asking people quality related questions. When they answer correctly, the associate receives a pencil with a quality logo inscribed on it. Quality related questions can include "what is our vision?," "what is our mission?," "what are our values?" along with high level quality questions.

Result: Fun! Employees engaged in thinking about quality.

Quality Scavenger Hunt

Submitted by: Debbie Brigham, Director of Quality, Glenayre.

Season: October,
National Quality Month.

Serves: Any number of teams of 4 - 6.

Ingredients: A list of 25 "test" questions related to the Quality Department, reproduced for the number of participants.

Directions: Give each team member a list of 25 quality related "test" questions. Each team hunts for the answers. An example would be, "Find the title to procedure #." The team to answer or "find" the most correct answers will be the winners. Each team member will receive a Star key chain.

Columbus Day, Sail into the Unknown

Submitted by: Lynnette Younggren

Season: October.

Serves: An organization or department.

Ingredients: A large supply of small tokens of recognition.

Directions: Recognize people who have taken risks, gone into unknown territory or been innovative. Co-workers and managers can recognize a "Columbus" and present him or her with a small token of recognition.

Trick or Treat

Submitted by: Susan Galloway, Training Manager, Navigant International. This is an old "family" recipe, so to speak, that originated with the front line staff many years ago.

Season: October, Halloween.

Serves: A small organization or department.

Ingredients: Candy, costumes, kids, a camera, a group of judges.

Directions: Encourage people in your organization to dress in costumes and bring candy to have at their desk. Invite anyone with children to have someone bring them in to roam the office collecting treats. Have the judging staff visit all locations and take pictures of groups or teams of people. At the end of the day, they chose a number of "best" dressed. You could even have several categories. The next day, display the photos and announce the winners. Put photos of the winners in your newsletter.

The Gift of Thanks for Giving

Submitted by: Kathe Farris, BankBoston

Season: Thanksgiving.

Serves: Small gathering.

Ingredients: Small note cards or Pocket Praise, beverages, snacks (optional).

Directions: Invite associates to a small gathering. In the invitation, include a bundle of small note cards or Pocket Praise.

The Twelve Days of Christmas

Submitted by: Baudville Creative Staff.

Season: Christmas.

Purpose: To honor department managers.

Serves: 25 - 100 people.

Ingredients: Creativity, a fun spirit. Props – felt Santa hats and tagboard.

Directions: Each department creates an activity or object to playfully honor their department manager. For example, during Baudville's 1998 Christmas party, each department got together to create a fun "thank you" for their manager. Working together as a team, the Customer Service Department modified the Twelve Days of Christmas song. Each verse related to their manager Karen's work style and personality. Karen is the most enthusiastic person you could ever meet. She is always smiling and laughing. To liven the delivery, each person wore a Santa hat, used props and acted out a part. One person played the role of conductor, using a candy cane as a baton and prompt cards on his chest. We don't want to keep you in suspense any longer. Here are the words:

On the First day of Christmas, Karen gave to me…a warm smile and howdy.

On the Second day of Christmas Karen gave to me…two thumbs up.

On the Third day of Christmas, Karen gave to me…three kind words.

On the Fourth day of Christmas, Karen gave to me…four questions answered.

On the Fifth day of Christmas, Karen gave to me…Five golden smiles.

On the Sixth day of Christmas, Karen gave to me…Six packs of post-its.

On the Seventh day of Christmas, Karen gave to me…Seven 'great job' cards.

On the Eighth day of Christmas, Karen gave to me…Eights calls a 'holdin.

On the Ninth day of Christmas, Karen gave to me…Nine 'how's it going?

On the Tenth day of Christmas, Karen gave to me…Ten sheets of labels.

On the Eleventh day of Christmas, Karen gave to me…Eleven stacks of purchase orders.

On the Twelfth day of Christmas, Karen gave to me…Twelve pages of corrections.

Results: A manager that felt moved to tears of joy and gratitude and a team that felt the joy of working on a project together.

The Gift of Giving Appreciation

Submitted by: Baudville Creative Staff.

Season: December, Hanukkah, Christmas, Kwanzaa.

Serves: Organization, small business or departments.

Ingredients: Baudville gift bags or small gift boxes, individual coffee, tea or cocoa pouches, chocolate coins, mini candy canes, a holiday border post card, tissue paper.

Directions: Prepare as many small gift bags (or boxes) as you have employees. Distribute one to each employee. Draw names. Each employee writes a note of appreciation to the co-worker whose name they drew and then presents that person the gift.

Sharing Tree

Submitted by: Liz Milo, Motivationery.

Season: The Holidays.

Serves: Your community.

Ingredients: One artificial holiday tree to give away, lights and a group of caring people.

Directions: Place the tree – bare except for lights – in your building's lobby or breakroom. Explain that the tree will be a gift to a needy family who cannot afford to provide one for their children. Invite employees to decorate the tree with ornaments that they are willing to contribute to the family. The real beauty of the tree is not how lovely it looks after it is outfitted with ornaments, but the symbolism of the tree and the spirit of giving it represents.

Memory Lane

Submitted by: Lorna Schreck, Optical Coating Labs, Inc.

Event: Celebration of organization's 50th anniversary.

Serves: An organization.

Ingredients: Company memorabilia, creativity, volunteer time.

Directions: We combined a 50th anniversary celebration with our annual picnic. People put together a "memory lane" of the company history with pictures, storyboards and equipment. Our first forklift was displayed. It was like a mini-museum, showing one decade at a time as folks walked through. Each department was encouraged to create a display in their production area showing products and processes. For instance, one of our departments showed how they accomplished their safety mission.

The picnic: We hired a company to cater the food and provide entertainment. We selected games for the children' including a Velcro bungee jump. There was a live band as well as Karioke. We even had a "misting station" to keep people cool.

Inviting Guests

How To Get Program Participation

ow would you feel if you planned a party and nobody came? Or, only a few guests showed up? Can you imagine the low energy level you and those attending would feel? Your guests look around and see a feast for 40 being served to ten. You've worked hard, spent many creative hours planning, cooking and cleaning. We don't want that to happen to you as you stage your recognition program. So be proactive – examine what causes poor participation and take actions to prevent it.

In order to get good program participation, your audience needs to:

• Know about it – what it is, why you're doing it.

• Commit to it.

• Know what to do.

• Feel comfortable doing it.

• Think it is easy.

Principle #1: Know About It

Lack of communication lies at the heart of many types of failures. When it comes to building a culture that thrives on recognition, communication helps people:

• Know what the program is all about.

• Know how to participate.

• Gain enthusiasm as participants.

• Congratulate others on their achievements – increasing the recognition's positive effects across the board.

 The Director of Human Resources at Freedom Village says about recognition, "It's a philosophy. Human Resources has to live it every day. We talk about it all the time. We bring up it in management meetings. We build momentum this way."

Kathe Farris of BankBoston says, "If you can, incorporate your communication (messages, marketing) into vehicles that already exist in your company. This is tremendously helpful when trying to ingrain this program into the culture and align it with the vision of the company."

 Sue Galloway, Training Manager at Navigant International, says, "The key to a successful roll-out is face-to-face communication from the immediate supervisor. By involving all people who have people reporting to them in this phase, you also build commitment and understanding. They are more likely to model positive recognition-giving behaviors."

 Communication comes in many forms. Determine the forms of communication available to you in your company and use them. For example, AT&T Universal Cards quarterly newsletter, "Applause," was devoted solely to employee recognition. It contained stories about people, service awards and how to participate in each program.

Common Corporate Communication Vehicles:

- Department meetings
- Town hall meetings
- Newsletters
- E-mail
- Flyers at entrances
- Table-tents in break rooms and lunch tables
- Posters
- Bulletin boards
- Traveling carts/kiosks
- Memos
- Closed circuit TV
- Video
- Inserts in paychecks
- Voice mail
- Home mailers

Get people's attention. Persuade them to get on the recognition-giving band-wagon. Encourage each and every employee, at each and every level, to be an internal salesperson for recognition.

Hints For Getting Your Ideas Across:

- Get their attention. Have a kickoff celebration.
- Tell them WIIFM benefits (What's In It for Them).
- Make the message clear and simple to understand.
- Give the message frequently – be in front of them often, repeating the same message.
- Allow time for germination – give time for the idea to take root and grow.
- Don't take a lot of their time: "Be brief, be bright, be gone." (Nancy Skinner, Nancy Skinner and Associates)
- Ask people for their ideas. We own what we create.
- Give people credit for ideas they contribute.
- Link the recognition program to other happenings.
- Be visible.

Plan Your Campaign:

What?	Where?	When?	Who's Responsible?

Principle #2: Commit to It

Before people can commit to the recognition program and before they will agree to expend time and energy on recognition, they must be aware of the need for it. Then, they must have the desire to participate. Desire may come from the awareness of WHY recognition is a good idea (as well as WIIFM – What's In It for Me?). When a person receives praise, there certainly is something in it for them. Use your communication tools and training sessions to help others see what's in it for them.

A very real way to increase commitment is by getting people involved. We are more likely to commit to things of which we are a part of. Ask people to participate in sessions that generate recognition program ideas and ask their opinion on what they would like to be recognized for. Include employees from all levels, shifts and every location.

Involve front-line leaders early on in the process. Having their commitment will do wonders for the commitment of people working for them. If the leader isn't committed, the followers are much less likely to commit.

Recognize recognition givers. They serve as your role models for others. They are doing what you want others to do – giving recognition. This is behavior you want repeated. How do you recognize their positive behavior? Give them a token reward that ties in with your purpose.

Turn their commitment to recognition into a habit of recognition.
To create a new habit, an individual must have:

- Awareness
- Desire
- Commitment
- Practice (repetition)

Ken Blanchard and Spencer Johnson in *The One Minute Manager* coined the phrase "Catch them doing something right." Start your recognition program off with a big flash! Give everyone in the company a disposable camera. Ask everyone to keep their eyes open and their camera ready to catch people doing something right. This could represent their "capturing the moment," or "seeing the best in people." Ask them to turn the cameras in and have the pictured developed. Publish the pictures in the company newsletter or post them on the wall, on a bulletin board or on the company's web site in a "Recognition Givers Hall of Fame." Then, sit back and watch your co-workers bask in the glory.

"A good program poorly communicated is much worse than a mediocre program well communicated"

Gillian Flynn
Workforce, July '98

Principle #3: Know What To Do

Here's a basic management rule: let others know what you expect of them.

Not knowing what to do or where to start can be a huge obstacle, no matter what you're trying to accomplish.

Once your program is up and running, use your communication vehicles to acknowledge people who have received recognition. Communicate clearly why each person received the recognition. Be very specific about the behaviors you are recognizing or rewarding. This will help the rest of the work-force understand what to recognize and will give them courage and inspiration. Living examples are the greatest teacher. To reinforce your communication, set up a Q and A section in your newsletter or as an email memo answering questions people have about what behaviors should be recognized and how to give recognition.

Principle #4: Feel Comfortable Doing It

Another obstacle to action, that squeamish feeling – call it shyness, a feeling of incompetence or a fear of failure – can keep people from participating in a recognition program. They need to feel comfortable giving as well as comfortable receiving recognition for your program to be a success.

Training can increase that comfort level. Training gives people knowledge about the program, shows them what's in it for them, tells them what to do, answers their questions and gives them practice. If training takes place in a fun atmosphere, they'll be eager to try recognition in the "real world."

Providing ready-to-use materials can also reduce discomfort with giving recognition. People who have trouble expressing themselves, in writing or verbally, may find it easy to hand out a Pocket Praise card or preprinted Thank You Post-It note that they simply sign and drop off. This makes recognition giving easier, too. How many times have you been so busy that you put off writing a note to someone? A small preprinted card or note would have taken you just 30 seconds.

When recognition giving becomes a comfortable activity, you're well on your way to making it fun and meaningful within your organization.

Principle #5: Think It Is Easy

You've been spending a great deal of time and thought on your recognition program. So… how can you make recognition giving easy?

First, make the process of getting recognition supplies easy. If you decentralize, set up a budget for each department and empower managers to design and implement their own programs with a few guidelines.

A company in Ohio sends a recognition kit to managers every four months. One might call this a "tickler service." If you don't want to hassle with putting kits together, try Baudville's Recognition FUNdamentals Kits. They contain an assortment of recognition-giving supplies. The deluxe kits even include software for making award certificates and coupons.

If you want award certificates to be part of your recognition program, load award-making software on a computer and keep award border papers available – for formal, casual or even humorous awards.

For spontaneous, creative and fun recognition, stock a "Trinkets and Treasures Chest" with silly, inexpensive items. It's the meaning behind the object that is important. And, fun items can create great memory value. Collect the items by asking for white elephant donations from the staff or make a trip to a dollar store. Include some TEAM Lifesavers®, Praise Pop suckers and motivational stickers. The mere activity of creating your Trinkets & Treasures Chest will motivate some to get busy in the business of recognition.

Motorola exemplifies "make it easy."

Motorola's 3,000 employee location in Plantation, Florida, has an employee store which fills the role of supplier for recognition items. The store makes it easy for peers to be spontaneous while making each other feel important. They can purchase birthday cards, balloons, gifts under $10, or collectibles like Beanie Babies® and Precious Moments®. Jean Ames, manager of the employee store, stocks a whole range of items like gift certificates and theme park, movie and sporting events tickets that managers use to further recognize and motivate their staff.

The company also makes it easy to give recognition by assigning a monthly recognition budget to each manager.

Motorola uses the recognition program to thank people for working extra long to meet shipping dates, which in turn makes happy customers. Recently, a manager wanted to thank his staff for working 80 hour weeks, 5 weeks in a row in order to meet deadlines. He rented a bus and took his staff of 36 to Universal Studios for a day. In addition to showing appreciation, this fun adventure built team camaraderie.

Another manager encouraged his staff to work extra hours by raffling off a television and VCR he purchased in the employee store. When people worked extra hours, they received a raffle ticket.

Managers learn of the items stocked in the employee store via the company newsletter and e-mail announcements.

Zeeland Community Hospital's Connect Card

Zeeland Community Hospital, a 405 employee hospital in Zeeland, Michigan, makes one of their recognition tools both visible and easy. "Connect Cards" are displayed in attractive, clear, hard plastic dispensers throughout the hospital. A laminated instruction sheet next to the dispenser tells people how to use the cards. The Connect Card was designed with great care and thought for maximizing recognition giving.

Lori Bruins, Performance Improvement Coordinator, says, "We really wanted a mechanism that let employees take control of recognizing each other. If they see someone doing something particularly good, or beyond their job duties, they fill out a Connect Card."

The Connect Card has two perforated parts. Recognition givers fill out one half, describing the reason for the recognition and give it to the recipient. The recognition givers fill out the other half, noting their name and the name of the recipient and then give it to the recipient's manager. " It is the manager's responsibility to go to the person and say, 'I got this Connect Card. What did you get it for?' Managers think it's helpful because they don't always see this stuff," says Lori. "And, it gives the employee the opportunity to tell about the reason, to brag without initiating it." How do people know about the Connect Card, other than seeing them in their rack?

"When the program started and now, during new employee orientation, the Connect Card is demonstrated and discussed," says Lori.

CalPERS "Top Ten"

Ideas don't always come easily. CalPERS (California Public Employees Retirement System) serves up a smorgasbord of ideas. They internally publish a list of the Top Ten Recognition Ideas. Here are three of them:

• Start or end staff meetings with "Recognition Moments." Encourage staff to share recognition stories.

• Make a phone call or send a note or letter to a staff member's family. Share how great the person is and how much you enjoy working with them.

• Make people a part of your to-do list.

A Credit Union Makes Change

Instead of using reward coupons, San Antonio Teachers Credit Union presents colorful plastic coins in ten denominations: 1 free soda, 1/2 day off, 1 candy bar, 1 early departure, 1 free lunch, 1 free staff shirt, 1 extended lunch, 1 lunch with the president of the company, 1 $25 gift certificate and recognition program points.

The supervisors receive a supply of the coins and use them to reward positive behaviors. During supervisory training on motivation and recognition, supervisors receive a tool kit with guidelines for when to use each reward. For example, give a free lunch for something like a, b, c, or d. Lisa Fairal, of the Training Department, says, "Our role is to give them the tools, and they can use what makes sense to their department. It doesn't need to be complicated or expensive, but it should be timely, creative and consistent. Our guidelines are: celebrate the successes; don't overlook the simplest form of praise – thank you; use praise and recognition to build employee loyalty and morale."

People are proud to receive the coins and even tape them to their computer, so their value exceeds "face value."

The checklist below will help you plan your actions and make sure you have covered your bases. Chapters 11 through 14 cover these topics in more depth, so you may prefer to finish reading the book and then return to this page.

Communicate/Invite

Who	Content	Format	When
	How are we going to communicate the program to everyone? What forms of media will we use?		Week 9
	What are our time lines?		
	Who will communicate face to face with staff?		
	Will we have a kickoff celebration? If not, how will we initiate the program?		
	What will we do to help people understand? What's In It for Them (WIIFT)?		
	How will we make sure people know what to do?		
	Will we have training? If so, for whom? Who will do it?		
	How will we recognize the recognizers?		
	How will we make sure people feel comfortable giving and receiving recognition?		
	How will we make the program easy to use?		
	Where will we keep supplies?		
	How will people obtain them?		

Determine "Who," "Format" and "When" based on the scope of your individual recognition initiative.

Map To The Party

Training Blazes An Easy Trail

CHAPTER 11

When people come to your house for the first time, do you draw them a map? That makes sense, doesn't it? You don't let your guests waste a lot of time trying to figure out the route, with the chance of getting lost. You simply give them a map. For some people, recognition is an undiscovered country. Make it easier for them. Give them a map – give them training.

What should your training workshop cover? Think of the six reporters' questions: why, who, what, when, where and how.

"REWARDS AND RECOGNITION PROGRAMS ARE ONLY AS GOOD AS EMPLOYEES' UNDERSTANDING OF THEM"

GILIAN FLYNN
WORKFORCE, JULY '98

Let's look at these reporter's questions in more depth...

Why? Discuss WIIFM (What's In It for Me). Talk about how the company, the manager and the individual benefit from recognition. Tie it into issues bigger than a warm, fuzzy people process. Include an introduction to motivation theories.

Who? Define who needs recognition and who will be responsible for giving recognition. As was discussed in Chapter 1, all people desire recognition. Who can also refer to: Who are you? – what is your recognition giving style? Who are your recipients and what recognition style will they appreciate most? Chapter 12 will help you answer these questions.

What? Define what behaviors will be recognized during your planning stages (as discussed in Chapter 4). Refine the "what" as you get feedback on your program.

When? Recognize during anniversaries, on holidays, during corporate events and whenever actions merit. Recognition is most effective when it is given immediately after the behavior took place.

Where and how to use the program will be guided by the resources you are supplying, the guidelines you give and the behavioral style of the giver and receiver (as discussed in Chapter 12). As you train people in recognition, let them know the importance of making it meaningful, having some fun and doing it now.

 During its recognition training workshops, a large corporation with branches throughout the country has facilitators lead the half-day workshops which involve supervisors and managers in activities that demonstrate how to value, motivate and recognize associates. During training, people are shown the reason for recognizing and valuing associates, practice the skills, use the tools and then learn ideas about giving recognition. The leader of this recognition training initiative noted that supervisors and managers are sent a bag of recognition supplies at intervals throughout the year. This keeps the ball rolling, reinforces recognition-giving behavior and provides the tools.

 San Antonio Teachers Credit Union also provides supervisory training on motivation and recognition. This organization – with 220 employee and six locations – trained 30 supervisors from vice presidents to front line. Lisa Fairall explains that the training helps supervisors understand why recognition is important and what the company is trying to accomplish. Lessons on how to create a motivational climate are demonstrated. Participants receive a "gold star goodie bag" filled with recognition tools — Pocket Praise, gift certificates from video stores and local grocery stores, a calendar with motivational sayings and ideas, and coin tokens. The agenda explains how and when to use the tokens. Additional resources such as book titles and web sites are included. The Credit Union refills recognition tool kits with resources quarterly.

Liz Milo said, "One question received quite a bit throughout my company, at least initially, was, 'What is appropriate to recognize?' Some people wanted a desired attribute to be defined as a specific behavior. The answer lies not with a formula, but with the empowerment of the work force that is sharing the recognition. It's a lot less important to control them, than to energize them."

Questions and Answers

Q. What topics should we discuss during training sessions?

A. Ask yourselves these questions:

• What is appropriate to recognize?

• To what degree does this attribute (such as initiative) need to be exhibited for me to recognize the person?

• When would you recognize someone for exemplifying this attribute (such as dedication)?

• How would an attribute like "teamwork" be defined?

• How would you use this recognition tool?

Q. What are some particular methods for use in training workshops?

A. Make it "active" training: people practice what you're asking them to do after they leave the session:

• Include fun and engaging activities that illustrate the benefits of recognition.

• Facilitate discussion to uncover fears and answer questions. After a positive atmosphere has been created in the session, your participants will be more likely to share their fears and objections.

• Encourage participants to talk about what isn't clear to them so it becomes more defined. To move forward on anything, we need to know what to do.

- Ask participants to share success stories in giving and receiving recognition.

- Give participants recognition supplies so they can apply what they have learned immediately.

Q. Who should be included in training?

A. That depends on your program. Definitely include anyone who has people reporting to them. If you're using day-to-day recognition as the core of the program, include everyone. Mix people up as far as levels and positions. This lets them hear each other's stories and can be good for team building as an added benefit. Include top management staff, too.

Q. I've seen people go to training, apply what they learned for a short time and then forget it. How do you make training stick?

A. Simple. Don't stop with the training. Follow up with a small reminder within two weeks – something like mini Life Saver rolls would be perfect. You're trying to create a new habit, so this early reminder is important. Send out a new bag of recognition tools within four months. This could include recognition Post-it notes or Pocket Praise.

By giving your guests a map, you increase program participation and success. As discussed in Chapter 10, your participants:

- Know about the program.

- Commit to it.

- Know what to do.

- Feel comfortable with it.

- Think it's easy to use.

Here's a sample recognition program training workshop...

Train

Who	Content	Format	When
	Interview and appreciate each other.	Activity	Weeks 10.11.12
	What is recognition?	Discussion	
	Why is the company supporting a recognition program?	Telling	
	WIIFM - What's In It for You?	Activity	
	Reinforcement Theory.	Telling and Activity	
	Who to recognize.	Reflection	
	What does our recognition program consist of?	Telling	
	When should recognition be given?	Telling and Activity	
	How to give recognition… Styles – make it meaningful, make it fun.	Practice and Activity	
	How to get supplies.	Telling	
	How to recognize recognition givers.	Discussion and Telling	

Determine the "Who" and "When" based on the scope
of your individual recognition initiative.

What To Wear

Make It Comfortable

Style can be everything. Take a dinner party, for example. Some are the casual, blue jeans type; some are business attire; some require black tie and formal length dresses. People feel uncomfortable if they are over-or under-dressed. They feel most comfortable when dressed appropriately.

In this chapter we will talk about:

- Understanding behavioral styles – the styles of the recognition giver and recognition receiver.

- Utilizing styles different from your natural styles (sort of like going from blue jeans to a tuxedo).

- Becoming comfortable giving and receiving recognition by learning about it in a training setting where there are opportunities to practice.

Where are you on the recognition-giving comfort scale?

I feel very awkward telling someone   I feel very comfortable telling someone
they did a good job, praising them.   they did a good job, praising them.

Questions and Answers

Q. I feel awkward giving recognition. What's wrong with me? What should I do?

A. Most people feel awkward when they try something new. For some, giving recognition is new. We suggest you:

- Acknowledge your discomfort.

- Examine how your natural "style" affects this.

- Learn how to give recognition from someone who is good at it.

- Practice in a safe setting.

- Practice, practice, practice with people who deserve to be thanked, praised, and acknowledged.

Q. How do I start a recognition-giving conversation? Sometimes it's starting the recognition conversation that stops me. I stumble over my words and feel awkward. What should I say?

A. Follow this Recognition Giving Recipe:*

- Thank the person, by name.

- Specifically state what was done that is being recognized.

- Explain how the behavior made you feel.

- Point out the value added to the team or company by the behavior.

- Thank the person by name, again, for his or her contribution.

- Keep it pure. Approach the person just for the reason of giving them a thank you, praise or acknowledgment.

For example,

"Roger, thank you for keeping our meeting on track by using an agenda. I felt productive because we accomplished our goals. The rest of the team and the company benefits from your meeting management skills. Thank you for your contribution, Roger."

*Joan Klubnik, *Rewarding and Recognizing Employees.* ©1995, Irwin Professional Publishing. Reproduced with permission of The McGraw-Hill Companies.

Keep it simple. It comes across more sincerely. Flowery vocabulary or excessive flattery can be interpreted as insincerity.

Q. I notice that some people act very shy when I thank or praise them. Why is this? What should I do?

A. Your recognition giving style is probably linked to your personal style, how much you like to receive recognition, your comfort with giving recognition and the role models you've had in your life. Use the Recognition Styles chart below to determine the kinds of recognition your recipients will be comfortable receiving.

Recognition Styles

	Comfortable giving recognition	Reluctant to give recognition
Outgoing, Extrovert	Easy Giver	Resistant Giver
Shy, Introvert	Quiet Giver	Seldom Giver

You may already know your giving style. If not, complete the activity on the following page. Check the box for each word in both columns that fits your style at work.

Words that might describe:	The Easy Giver and The Quiet Giver	The Resistant Giver and The Seldom Giver
	☐ Caring	☐ Reserved
	☐ Feeling	☐ Thinking
	☐ Harmony	☐ Critical
	☐ Personal	☐ Impersonal
	☐ Tactful	☐ Direct
	☐ Gentle	☐ Firm
	☐ Empathetic	☐ Analyzer
	☐ Warm-hearted	☐ Matter-of-fact
	☐ Enthusiastic	☐ Decisive
	☐ Trusting	☐ Self-assured
	☐ Sociable	☐ Accurate
	☐ Patient	☐ Perfectionist
	☐ Agreeable	☐ Well-disciplined
	☐ Friendly	☐ Thorough
	☐ Talkative	☐ Logical
	☐ Quiet	☐ Systematic
	☐ Accepting	☐ Results-oriented
	☐ Cheerleader	☐ Problem-solver

Total for column _____   _____

Which column has more words checked? What kind of recognition-giving style do you use? If you desire to increase your recognition giving and you commit to doing so, learn more about your giving style options. Start with what is most comfortable to you. Then expand your comfort zone to start giving in the style of the receiver. Use this same list to assess others giving and receiving styles. Introverts usually like to give recognition in a private setting, extroverts in a public setting. In order to adapt to others styles, take these four steps.

1. Become aware

2. Develop a desire

3. Make a commitment

4. Practice.

Receiving recognition in a private setting will be appreciated by most anyone. Receiving recognition in a public setting can cause major discomfort for an introvert. If you're an "Easy Giver," please take care to observe the style of the receiver. This will help you avoid an awkward moment that could possibly negate the value of the recognition.

'PAUSE BEFORE YOU APPLAUD.'

Easy Givers and Quiet Givers usually choose a more casual, personal format while Resistant Givers and Seldom Givers choose a more formal, impersonal format. Easy Givers and Quiet Givers tend to be more "people-oriented" people while Resistant Givers and Seldom Givers tend to be "task-oriented" people. For task-oriented people, formality often feels more comfortable.

The bottom line – positively reinforcing behaviors that help achieve the desired results can work wonders for you, your company and the individual receiving recognition. So act now. Utilize the above tools to be more effective.

Just as you have your own "style" in giving recognition, people have their own desired "style" for receiving recognition. Be aware of the style others prefer, respect their preference and act accordingly. Use this chart to determine what types of recognition receivers you'll be recognizing.

Where are your recipients on the recognition-receiving comfort scale?

	Likes to receive recognition	Doesn't like to receive recognition
Outgoing, Extrovert	Enthusiastic Receiver	Low-Key Receiver
Shy, Introvert	Modest Receiver	Private Receiver

Ideas for recognition giving vehicles by receiving style:

Enthusiastic Receiver	Modest Receiver	Low-Key Receiver	Private Receiver
Fun object	Sticky note	Handshake	Sticky note
Balloons	Thank you note	Note in the newsletter	Thank you note
Humorous award certificate	Flower from garden	Formal thank you at a team meeting	Formal award certificate
Food for a group	Homemade cookies	Take the person to lunch	Card with pre-printed verse

While your recognition "vehicles" should relate to personal style, the method or setting is equally important. You may think you have planned a delightful experience, but it might turn into a disaster if you don't consider the receiver's style. In sum, outgoing extroverts feel comfortable with public recognition. The Enthusiastic Receiver enjoys public acknowledgments that offer a lot of fanfare and celebration. However, low-key and private receivers are particularly critical of gushiness. They probably will interpret it as insincerity.

To determine what setting people prefer for receiving recognition, ask! Simply use the "Tell Us About You" recognition registry (Chapter 19, Ready to Use Forms) and you'll have the answer.

If your recipient looks uncomfortable when you're saying thank you or offering praise, be an aware recognition giver. Watch the person you're recognizing for signs of embarrassment. Keep it brief, tone it down. They are sending you a clear signal that this is not easy for them. But don't avoid giving them recognition in the future. Just remember to keep it brief or use a less direct method like a written note or e-mail. Sometimes the written format can be very effective because the person can read it over and over and receive the positive effect again and again.

"DON'T GO ON AND ON WITH A PERSON WHO IS VISIBLY UNCOMFORTABLE WITH REINFORCEMENT. A SPECIFIC COMMENT ON SOMETHING THEY DID, A PAT ON THE BACK, A THUMBS-UP SIGN, A WINK ACROSS THE ROOM, OR A SMILE WILL DO. THE BEST REINFORCEMENT IN THIS CASE IS SOMETHING THAT ONLY TAKES A FEW SECONDS TO SEND AND RECEIVE.."

JANIS ALLEN WITH GAIL SNYDER
I Saw What You Did & I Know Who You Are

If the people you're recognizing don't seem to believe you, ask yourself this question: Have you been giving recognition regularly for some time? If not, people may not "believe" your new behavior at first. Keep giving sincere, timely, specific recognition. In time they will start trusting that your behavior is sincere.

Knowing what you know now, let's help you avoid recognition giving pitfalls.

Make It Personal

What is your giving style?

_____

What actions that you take might cause discomfort or annoyance or miss the maximum effectiveness with different styles?

Receiving Style:	Action
Enthusiastic Receiver	_____
Modest Receiver	_____
Low-key Receiver	_____
Private Receiver	_____

Return to Chapter 1 to review the list of people you will be recognizing. List their names below and fill in the blanks on their apparent receiving style and how they might like to receive recognition.

Name	Receiving Style	How
_____	_____	_____
_____	_____	_____
_____	_____	_____
_____	_____	_____
_____	_____	_____

Receiving Style Key:
E = Enthusiastic
M = Modest
L = Low-key
P = Private

How Key:
K = Public
S = Semi-private
Q = Private (Quiet)

Favorite Foods

Make It Meaningful

CHAPTER 13

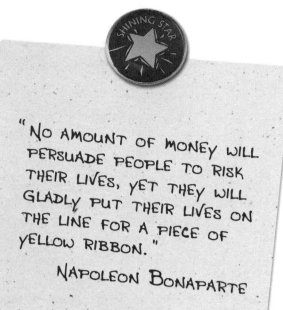

How many of you get to choose your favorite foods for your birthday dinner? Doesn't it make you feel special, like an honored guest? This chapter will help you choose the "just desserts" that make each person your program recognizes feel special. Why? Because you gave a reward that was meaningful to them.

Think about a time when someone gave you a gift that made you feel truly special. What was it? Why did it make you feel so special? Chances are, it was special because you knew it had been chosen just for you, not for just anyone.

"No amount of money will persuade people to risk their lives, yet they will gladly put their lives on the line for a piece of yellow ribbon."

Napoleon Bonaparte

When you think of making something meaningful, cover these two angles:

1. What does this person want to be recognized, praised or thanked for?

2. What would this person enjoy as a token of appreciation?

The "what fors" are the behaviors and results discussed in Chapter 4. These behaviors and results contribute to organizational goals. When it comes to thanking or acknowledging individuals for their specific efforts, you'll find many choices within your own organization's culture, goals and values.

Personal Reflection

What behaviors do you really value in yourself? What results are you proud of? List two or three accomplishments or traits you would like to be thanked or acknowledged for at work:

1._____
2._____
3._____

What would you consider a meaningful token of appreciation?
See Chapter 7 for ideas.

Under $5.00	$5 – $10.00	$10 – $20.00

BE A RECOGNITION DETECTIVE. TAKE PRIDE IN OBSERVING WHAT WOULD BE MEANINGFUL TO EACH PERSON. KEEP A PAGE IN YOUR PLANNER WITH NAME AND IDEAS.

Now, consider the people you want to recognize. What might be meaningful to them?

You may feel at a loss as to what to give someone. You want it to be meaningful, but you might miss the mark. Conducting a survey, like the sample Baudville "Tell Us About You Registry Card," can help ensure your success by making recognition meaningful. This survey card helps you identify the types of recognition and rewards your recipients will respond to most favorably.

As you work on the job, observe, listen and record ideas for meaningful recognition for the individuals you rub shoulders with. Keep a page in your planner labeled "Recognition Ideas."

We truly feel valued when someone does something that takes thought. For starters, think of one person you want to recognize. To get your mental mechanism moving, consider the person's hobbies and interests. Is family a high priority?

Where do you get these ideas? Talk to them. Observe their work area. Do they have personal photographs? Maybe a picture frame would be appreciated. Do they have sticky notes everywhere? Treat them to some recognition sticky notes. Do they bring their lunch to work? Buy them a special lunch bag.

Don't forget that non-tangible positive reinforcement can be equally fulfilling.

• Invite them to become a member of a team project.

• Ask them to coach, train or mentor a co-worker.

• Give them a job assignment that interests them.

• Encourage them to bring their children to work for a day.

 Michelle Montiel at Freedom Village, a Continuing Care Retirement Community, says, "Recognition is about the things you can do for your employees to let them know they matter. It's the little things that count. The little things make the job more appealing."

Freedom Village uses lots of verbal thank yous, lets staff go home early, come in late and use flex time as rewards. Freedom Village believes being flexible with people shows you care. Reward coupons are used to thank people for positive behaviors.

 Jackie Barnd, Walgreen Company, talks about how meaningful a certificate of completion can be. She oversees the company's Welfare to Work and School to Work programs which operate in Chicago, New Orleans, St. Louis, Cleveland and Cincinnati. This program teaches retailing and customer service skills to youths and adults in lower income areas. When they've finished the class, students attend a formal presentation where they very ceremoniously receive a certificate of completion, nestled in a nice presentation folder. Jackie says, "They have a great sense of pride. 'I learned something, and I have something to show for it.' They take it with them when they apply for a job. It can help them get a better job." Now that's meaningful!

 Scott Jones, Resident Coordinator at University of Miami, understands how important it is to make recognition meaningful. He strives to build camaraderie among his 27 resident assistants and retain them from year to year. His program, "Making People Matter," starts with a weekend retreat where he gets to know his staff. Activities include a workshop on personality traits and a ropes course event. This gives everyone a kick start on understanding what is important to others and what can be appreciated about others. Throughout the year, other events help the staff build teamwork. They explore Miami, schedule bowling nights, host barbeques and take a Cuban restaurant tour. Scott says, "Food is the biggest incentive."

If your staff works with the public, a name badge that shows how many years of service they have with the company can be meaningful. This offers customers an opportunity to comment with praise.

For a volunteer, a lapel pin commemorating their service can be meaningful. People who volunteer often do so because they want to help others. When they wear the pins, they open themselves up to positive comments about their service.

The measure of meaning you transfer to your rewards is only limited by your imagination and your power of observation. Once you begin discovering what's important to others, you may be surprised at your talents as a recognition detective. An added benefit, YOU will receive positive reinforcement every time you present a reward that delights your recipient.

Favorite Foods : **Make It Meaningful**

Personal Reflection: Recognition Detective Log

Make notes about people and their preferences:

Name	What do they value?	Hobbies, interests, likes	Ideas for recognition

Time To Eat

Make It Fun!

ow it's time to implement your program. Roll it out, one dish at a time. By offering one recognition activity at a time, you can savor the delicious results while gaining feedback before you offer the next. This will also make the process less confusing for you and those who are implementing the program activities. Too much great food at once can give you indigestion; too many great recognition activities at once diminish the positive effect.

WHEN PLATO WAS ASKED THE QUESTION, "WHAT THEN IS THE RIGHT WAY TO LIVE?" HIS REPLY WAS, "LIFE SHOULD BE LIVED AS PLAY."

Have fun with your programs. Design fun into them, have fun designing them and have fun experiencing them. Recognition should not feel like drudgery. People enjoy receiving recognition and you'll receive joy in giving recognition.

Many years ago my boss often overheard conversations I was having with my customers and said "Lynnette, you have too much fun at work!" My thoughts were "What's wrong with that? How can enthusiasm, energy and commitment to my customers be a bad thing?" I really put myself into my work because I love it, and it shows.

When you laugh, you massage the inside of your body. Try it. Laugh hearty and loud for one minute. Others will wonder what you're up to, but you'll feel uplifted. Imagine having a one minute laughing break once a day in your department. Shared laughter could be an energizing, bonding experience. Can you laugh and be tense at the same time?

Fun and recognition both spark positive responses inside a person. Both can also create energy and alertness. Both make people feel good. Fun doesn't need to include silliness and laughter. An event that's a special celebration can be fun in its own right.

An employee celebrating her twenty-year service anniversary received a catalog of gifts to choose from as her company's only token of gratitude. The gift arrived in the mail. Instead of feeling special and honored, this impersonal experience left her feeling that the company did not appreciate her decades of service.

This was a lost opportunity. Much of recognition's value comes from the celebration, whether public or private. The tangible gift reminds and relives the good feelings experienced during the celebration, and encourages its recipient to repeat the positive behavior. Think of all the ways you could make an anniversary commemoration more personal, more of a celebration. It could be as simple as the person's manager presenting the gift in front of the department. Review Chapter 8 for more ideas on employment anniversaries. Gift ideas are presented by price category and you'll find successful presentation methods used by other companies.

Questions and Answers

Q. Does recognition have to be fun in order to be effective?

A. No. Your recognition-giving can be a mix of the formal and the fun. Some people feel more comfortable with a fun, lively delivery of recognition while others appreciate a more serious, restrained delivery.

Q. If giving recognition used to be fun and energizing, but seems to have lost its zip, how do I revitalize it?

A. First, develop some new recognition activities. Programs that stay the same for a long time lose interest. After six months or a year, come up with some new activities. Look through our recipes. If you've only had a formal program, start an informal, peer-to-peer program. This will not only generate renewed interest, but also make recognition giving a daily occurrence that begins to transform the company culture. For another way to infuse your program with new energy, train everyone how to give recognition and give them each a "tool kit" of recognition supplies.

Q. Having fun at work benefits everyone. How do I convince others – especially top management?

A. Review the benefits:

- Job satisfaction

- Morale

- Productivity

- Creativity

The benefits of having fun at work and feeling good about what you're doing affects everyone working with you. If you have fun at work, work can become something you look forward to, like play. This can help your company to decrease absenteeism and turnover.

Q. How do I create fun at work and tie it in to recognition?

A. Draw from your resources – this book, other books on recognition, the Baudville and NAER (National Association of Employee Recognition) web sites, for example. Other resources are very close at hand. Get a group of people together to brainstorm ideas. You'll be amazed by what happens when people start bouncing ideas off each other.

As with any meeting, your brainstorming meeting should have the right people, a clear purpose, a time frame and an agenda. Be sure that agenda includes fun. Ask for volunteers or invite those who enjoy being creative. Not everyone feels comfortable when asked to be creative. Let this project be a benefit for someone who does.

Q. Where do we start?

A. As you plan your brainstorming meeting, remember the big picture purpose. Tie your brainstorming topics into higher company goals or values. For instance, if one of your values is Quality Work Environment, aim for fun recognition-giving ideas that will enhance the work environment and improve morale. If you have previously gone through the recommended process of linking your recognition program to higher company goals and values, you will already have your purpose defined.

" You get the best effort from others not by lighting a fire beneath them, but by building a fire within them."

Bob Nelson

Rewarding and Recognizing Employees

To make meetings fun, one company tapes a motivational saying or a happy face sticker to the bottom of three different chairs. At the start of the meeting, everyone looks under their chair. If they find a sticker, they share a recent career accomplishment and receive a prize. Prizes have ranged from motivational books to TEAM pencils, recognition Post-It notes or a bag of recognition tools. To spice it up, they sometimes have people draw their prize out of a bag. What a great way to get people to a meeting on time!

Meeting purpose:

Ask yourself these questions *and answer them...*

What do we recognize now?

_____

_____

_____

_____

What else could we recognize?

_____

_____

_____

_____

Using this list, choose the purpose for your meeting. You can either finely focus on one of the "whats" or you can tackle the whole list.

If you recognize anniversary dates with the company, state the meeting's purpose to be: we will find ways to make anniversary date acknowledgment more fun, lively and meaningful.

Or... start from the other side. Find some products in a recognition supply catalog and use them as a catalyst for ideas.

Purpose:

Brainstorm a list of ways these products could be used to make giving recognition more fun. Break group into teams of two to four people. Give each team one product to brainstorm. As each team "reports back," the other teams could add more ideas. For example:

Product: PhotoFrame – a picture frame made with border paper for four-by-six inch photos. *Idea:* post photos of employees the week of their anniversary with the company.

Product: Snap Together Button. *Idea:* copy enough head-shot photos of the anniversary person to place within snap-together buttons for everyone in the department to wear for the day.

Review Chapter 5 for more fun recognition recipes.

Time Frame:

Always include a start time and stop time on your meeting agenda, and STICK with it!

Agenda:

If you don't know where you're going, how can you get there? Write it down, make copies and give one to everyone in advance. Assign one person the responsibility of keeping the meeting on schedule.

Creating Fun:

When brainstorming, set a short amount of time and break the group into teams. The short time creates pressure – and pressure can jump-start the creative process while having teams creates competition. Give the team generating the most ideas a reward. Hand out TEAM Lifesavers. Don't worry about evaluating quality. The point is to get ideas flowing and to have fun!

The recognition staff at St. Francis Hospital & Health Services in Maryville, Missouri, knows how to make employee recognition fun. Gail Ingram related how they have a special event, Heritage Days Retreat, to show appreciation. The St. Francis team enjoys motivational speakers, door prizes, scavenger hunts and competitive games with prizes. Some of the founding sisters tell about the hospital's history. To ensure participation, team members attending are paid for their time and can choose from four different dates. Everyone can attend because they have coverage for their departments.

St. Francis does not stop here. Last year they had another special "Thank You Staff" event. Each shift could attend a noon picnic, a beach party in January (complete with sand and tropical effects) or a breakfast. The fourteen-member Mission Awareness Team volunteers their time to plan and run these events as well as community service events.

Motorola, Plantation, Florida, has a tradition of recognizing people on their birthdays. They really activate fun and the "I see you" principle. Once one person knows of a birthday, they pin a one-dollar bill on the birthday person's shirt. As the day goes on, people add money so the birthday person walks around with a chain of money. Sometimes the bills added go as high as a ten. Wow! Isn't that the way to be recognized!

Motorola has also given out special collectible bottle caps and colored marbles worth different dollar values. The value ascribed to these items can be redeemed for gifts in the gift shop.

Questions and Answers

Q. Do I need to have a theme for my program?

A. No, but themes have positive advantages. Themes can convey and unite ideas, making them seem purposeful. They also add an element of fun. Try giving your program a name, a theme and coordinated graphics. Your program's identity can be a great rallying point for employees, giving higher purpose to their endeavors.

Q. How about using food as a recognition reward?

A. Great idea. Food items are most effective when they're used to recognize a particular achievement. A manager may even cater an appreciation lunch for the department to say thank you for meeting production or quality goals.

Implement

Who	Content	Format	When
	Ask "How are we going to make the delivery of this program fun, lively and energetic?"		
	Who are fun, creative people to invite to brainstorming sessions?		
	What order and timing are we going use to implement the programs?		
	Open your "doors" for recognition business. Be available to answer questions.		Week 12
	Keep your ears open.		
	Model the recognition behaviors you value.		
	Recognize the recognizers.		

Determine "Who," "Format" and "When" based on the scope of your individual recognition initiative.

Master Chef

A Quiz

CHAPTER 15

Test your own recognition expertise! Read the following case study and answer the questions following it. The answers are all in the book!

A large corporation's credit department celebrates in a big way. Once a year they have a celebration where award certificates are given to people who have hit goal, 11 out of 12 months of the year. This big meeting of fun and games includes managers, directors and 800 employees.

In the middle of the year, they recognize those individuals who are on their way and have hit 5 out of 6 months – who could possibly be an all-star at the end of the year. Achievers receive a "You are a Star" bag filled with a Celebration tumbler, Shining Star Post-It notes and note pads. This is definitely something individuals strive to earn. They want to be known for being an all-star because it's great for their career.

Each area has its own goals. Every month, people reaching their monthly goals are also recognized. Top performers – people way above everyone – receive special recognition. In addition, the corporation gives day-to-day and peer-to-peer recognition. When a person receives a customer's letter of commendation, the group gathers to celebrate by giving them a special gift and a laminated copy of the letter to display on their desk.

Also, peers can give commendations to each other. For instance, when an employee's work partner solved a customer problem she had been unsuccessful with, she shared the success at a department meeting and presented her work partner with a bag of goodies. The corporation also recognizes individuals for leadership and community service.

What makes the "All Star" process structured for success?

_____

_____

_____

What makes the day-to-day and peer-to-peer process structured for success?

_____

_____

_____

What makes the combination of the two successful?

_____

_____

_____

Will this program best work if you're Flying Solo? If you're on a Task Force? Or, if you're working as part of a Corporate Initiative?

_____

_____

_____

How would you "tweak" this program to fit your organization?

_____

_____

_____

Give yourself 1 point for each idea or each correct answer.

Reward yourself: 2-4 points, have a mini candy bar; 5 -7 points, a full size candy bar; 8-10 points, an ice cream cone; more than 10, go to your favorite restaurant for lunch. Adjust rewards to match your preferences. (Sorry, you have to provide your own rewards!)

Suggested Answers:

Q. What makes the "All Star" process structured for success?

A. Recognition is given each month, with bigger celebrations at six months and one year. This gives regular feedback to performers and can be very motivating. It also reminds people of goals and gives them a feeling of achievement on a regular basis. It recognizes smaller achievement on the path to larger goals, which gives encouragement. The recognition is presented in a setting of fun and celebration. Because the results are very visible, even to top management, the staff sees the recognition as helping their career goals. For career growth, one wants to be noticed.

Q. What makes the day-to-day and peer-to-peer process structured for success?

A. Celebrations happen on a regular basis. Employees know they are appreciated year 'round, not just once a year. Recognition is given close to the time when the achievement occurred.

Rewards are tangible. The certificate and gift bag can be displayed for others to see. The recognition goes on and on – not only because others can see the tangible items, but because the items remind the recipients of their achievement. The program also supports company goals.

Q. What makes the combination of the two successful?

A. Together, they recognize achievement of measurable results and reinforce behaviors that support company goals – customer satisfaction, teamwork and going above and beyond the call of duty. Some recognition is given in front of a large gathering of people, some within the more closely knit, work-group setting.

Q. Will this program best work if you're Flying Solo? If you're on a Task Force? Or, if you're working as part of a Corporate Initiative?

A. I would see this as a Corporate Initiative. It requires top management support, allows the figures to be shared and involves a substantial, although not extreme, commitment of dollars.

Q. How would you "tweak" this program to fit your organization?

A. Here's one I can't answer for you. However, it could be done on a smaller scale, in one department.

Congratulations! You're becoming a recognition expert.

Go forth and find ways to make recognition fun!

Feedback For The Cook

Comments From The Guests

CHAPTER 16

Feedback For The Cook: Comments From The Guests

Have you ever cooked a fabulous meal (or so you thought) and then not one of your guests commented? What did you think? "Maybe my meal was bad." "Maybe the meal wasn't something that fit their tastes." "Maybe my guests were having such a good time they forgot to comment on the meal." Receiving no feedback can be disconcerting.

In your recognition program, not gaining feedback is more than disconcerting, it's a death knell. You must have feedback in order to continue to receive support and funding. Only feedback can enable you to learn, improve and change your program to meet your company's needs.

We discussed tracking and measuring your recognition program's results in stage two of the nine-step process (Chapter 4).

Track/Measure

Who	Content	Format	When
	Set up a spreadsheet to record each program. Keep track of costs.		Week 13
	Re-administer the employee recognition satisfaction survey, do a random phone survey or host a focus group.		Week 40
	Produce a report showing results of the measurement indicators you decided to use in the strategic link phase (see Chapter 4).		Week 42
	Display results in fun, colorful ways.		
	Celebrate your success!		Week 42

Determine the "Who" and "Format" based on the scope of your individual recognition initiative.

Tracking lets you know that your program is being used. Kathe Farris says "Measurement overall is key in recognition programs. One of our more interesting measurements was that since September 1996, every three minutes someone was being recognized at BankBoston."

 Debbie Patrick, who was the Recognition and Employee Event/Involvement Manager for AT&T Universal Card Services for more than five years, says "I recommend everyone track their programs from the very beginning. Why? Because it's an excellent way to show the finance people and executives they are getting their money's worth, their return on investment. You need to link business results to the recognition programs."

AT&T went a few steps further. They did a data feed to accounting for tax purposes, and to corporate headquarters. One of the vice presidents of AT&T would send a letter each quarter to the home of everyone who had received a global award during that quarter.

On a scheduled basis, provide a concise report to the person who controls the recognition budget. Show results as the measurements you've tracked: employee satisfaction, attendance and customer satisfaction, to name a few.

Please, please don't forget to celebrate your success. This is another way to garner the continued support and involvement of the people who have helped make your program an initial success. Remember these two principles:

1. Feedback can be a source of energy.
2. We get what we reward.

Second Helpings

Make It A Habit

CHAPTER 17

Tweak/Troubleshoot

Who	Content	Format	When
Design Team	Examine the survey results and discuss ways to change and improve the program.		Week 42

Determine the "Format" based on the scope of your individual recognition initiative.

When people use a positive behavior that supports company mission and values one time, this is good – but not good enough to ensure success. If you put all your cake ingredients in the bowl and stirred them once, your cake would NOT be a success. You want people to use positive behaviors over and over again. You want people to make positive reinforcement a habit.

Defined as a usual manner of behavior, a habit is a behavior that occurs over and over, naturally and effortlessly. That's how you want recognition giving to occur. Although you want the gesture to be thoughtful, you also want the words of thanks and acknowledgments of efforts to come naturally to the lips of your staff.

Habits are Formed by Awareness, Desire, Commitment and Practice

Awareness. First, people must be exposed to the activity, become aware of it. Some people may never have considered saying thank you or acknowledging someone else's efforts or achievements. Expose them to the behavior (recognition-giving), let them see its benefits first-hand and move them on to the next step: desire. While you can't create desire inside of someone else, you can provide the catalyst. Let them know WIIFM (What's In It for Me).

By means of dialog, discussions or training sessions (Chapter 11), communicate why recognition giving will benefit the company and its employees. Ask managers to lead their staffs in discussions about recognition. When people discover the reasons themselves, the discovery will hold more meaning for them.

Training demonstrates that the company is committing time and money to the recognition program. It gives the program credibility by promoting it as a thoughtfully designed and communicated plan. Training works as a springboard for your recognition program because people tend to avoid activities if they don't feel they can do well or when they don't enjoy doing them. Training compares to a flight simulator– people can get the awkward first attempts out of the way in a safe environment. Also, something they've said or done once, comes more easily the second time.

Desire. Recognize the recognizers – publicly. Use bulletin boards, newsletters, e-mail and staff meetings. Publicly thank the people who are giving recognition. This identifies role models, praises achievement and establishes an "in crowd" that others will want to join. Enlist managers to evaluate recognition giving on performance reviews. Better yet, encourage them and other superiors to talk about it with employees on a regular basis. Jean Hand, Director of Customer Service at Super Vision International in Orlando, Florida, says, "Managers have standards and one of them is recognizing their employees."

Commitment. Commitment is built on desire, focus and purpose. Dennis C. Kinlaw, in his book *Coaching for Commitment,* says "Committed people know what they are doing, and they believe that what they are doing is important. People cannot become committed to what is vague or trivial."

To build commitment, let people know how recognition giving supports the vision and values of the company. This provides people a higher purpose. Show the company's commitment to recognition giving by engaging top level people to explain the program in a talk, newsletter or video presentation. Continually broadcast messages of support from the top.

Practice. Find as many ways as you can to say "Recognition-giving is important to the company." Involve people at ALL levels in the planning, training and executing processes. They'll be much more likely to commit to recognition giving if they feel they "own" the program.

If you're having trouble getting people on-board, make sure they know what is expected. Make sure they know how to do it – through training and mentoring. Give positive reinforcement. Praise them each time they give recognition, even in a small way.

" WHEN YOU CHOOSE A HABIT, YOU ALSO CHOOSE THE RESULT."

ZIG ZIGLAR

Work hard to gain the support of people who are admired by others. They have referent power – others want to follow them.

Some recognition programs seem to become entitlements. People feel that rewards received will keep coming, no matter what. To prevent this from happening to your program, change the activities regularly, keep the rewards' dollar value minimal and concentrate on day-to-day, peer-to-peer recognition as your primary recognition vehicle.

Ensure your program's results by helping people develop habits– habits that achieve your organization's goals for recognition.

Go forth and realize the joy of recognition!

Deli Foods

Ready To Use Forms

CHAPTER 18

Pre-Launch Recognition Survey

Rate the following on a scale of 1 - 5.

1 = Strongly Disagree, 5 = Strongly Agree

I receive timely and meaningful recognition when I exceed expectations or go above and beyond in my work (use past six months as benchmark reference).

1   2   3   4   5

Comments: _____

_____

I receive frequent feedback about how I am doing in my job.

1   2   3   4   5

Comments: _____

_____

I feel appreciated for the work I do.

1   2   3   4   5

Comments: _____

_____

I am satisfied with the amount of recognition I receive for my efforts.

1   2   3   4   5

Comments: _____

_____

I receive recognition for my efforts at work from the person I report to.

1   2   3   4   5

Comments: _____

_____

I receive recognition for my efforts at work from co-workers.

1   2   3   4   5

Comments: _____

_____

I give recognition to the person I report to for his/her efforts.

1   2   3   4   5

Comments: _____

_____

I give my co-workers recognition for their efforts.

1   2   3   4   5

Comments: _____

_____

I tend to perform better when I understand how my work contributes to the company and feel that my efforts are appreciated.

1   2   3   4   5

Comments: _____

_____

Shopping List

Your Recognition Pantry

CHAPTER 19

Books

I Saw What You Did and I Know Who You Are: Bloopers, Blunders, and Success Stories on Giving and Receiving Recognition. Janis Allen with Gail Snyder, 1990.
Phone: 828-862-6552, janisallen@yahoo.com

You Made My Day: Co-worker Recognition and Relationship. Janis Allen and Michael McCarthy, 2000.
Phone: 828-862-6552, janisallen@yahoo.com

Workplace Recognition: Step-by-step Examples of a Positive Reinforcement Strategy. Sue Glasscock & Kimberly Gram, 1999.

See Bibliography for additional titles.

Audiocassettes

Janis Allen on Recognition: What Everyone Who Works with People Needs to Know, 1993.
Phone: 828-862-6552,
janisallen@yahoo.com

Recognition Support Contacts

Baudville Inc.
800- 728-0888
www.baudville.com

Lynnette Younggren, TEAM
616-949-7976
team@voyager.net

Debra Sikanas, President
Baudville, Inc.
800-728-0888
debras@baudville.com

N.A.E.R.
National Association for Employee Recognition*
630-369-7783
www.recognition.org

*NAER is a nonprofit organization dedicated to the enhancement of employee performance through recognition, including its strategies and related initiatives. The association provides a forum for information and best practices sharing as well as education to foster the use, excitement, effectiveness and enthusiasm for recognition.

Organizational Contributors

BankBoston, Kathe Farris, Boston, MA

Baudville, Inc., Diane Newton, Grand Rapids, MI

CalPERS, Debbie Bennett, Heidi Evans, Sacramento, CA

City of Woodville, John Griswold, Woodville, NH

First Nationwide Mortgage, Eva Parker, Brea, CA

Freedom Village, Michelle Montiel, Braydenton, FL

Gillette Company, Rose Landre, Santa Monica, CA

Glenayre, Debbie Brigham,Quincy, IL

Grand Rapids Community College, Richard Austin, Grand Rapids, MI

Horizons Community School, Stelle Slootmaker, Wyoming, MI

Meijer, Inc., Pam Bell, Walker, MI

Miami University, Scott Jones, Miami, FL

Motivationery, Liz Milo, Jacksonville, FL

Motorola, Jean Ames, Fort Lauderdale, FL

Navigant International, Susan Galloway, Grand Rapids, MI

Navy Personnel Command, MWR Training Branch, Millington, TN

OMS, Jill Lindemoen, Fargo, ND

Optical Coating Labs, Inc., Lorna Schreck, Santa Rosa, CA

PNC Bank , Darliene Townsend, Pittsburgh, PA

Debbie Patrick, Kissimmee, FL

Shopping List: Your Recognition Pantry

Porter Hill Presbyterian Village, Sherri Bradford Royle, Grand Rapids, MI

San Antonio Teachers' Credit Union, Lisa Fairal, San Antonio, TX

St. Francis Hospital, Gail Ingram, Maryville, MO

Super Vision, International, Jean Hand, Orlando, FL

Walgreen Company, Jackie Barnd, Deerfield, IL

Zeeland Community Hospital, Lori Bruins, Zeeland, MI

Bibliography

Allen, Janis with Snyder, Gail. *I Saw What You Did and I Know Who You Are: Bloopers, Blunders and Success Stories on Giving and Receiving Recognition.* Tucker, GA: Performance Management Publications, 1990.

Baker, Dr. Larry, and Douglas, Dr. Merrill, *Time Mastery Facilitators Kit.* Carlson Learning Company, 1993.

Bell, Chip R. and Zemke, Ron. *Managing Knock Your Socks Off Service.* New York: Berkley Books, 1992.

Berry, Leonard L., and Parasuraman, A. *Marketing Services: Competing Through Quality.* New York: The Free Press, 1991.

Blanchard, Dr. Kenneth and Johnson, Dr. Spencer. *The One Minute Manager.* New York: Berkley Books, 1981.

Blanchard, Ken and Bowles, Sheldon. *Gung Ho!* New York: William Morrow & Company, 1997.

Boyle, Daniel C. *Secrets of a Successful Employee Recognition System.* Productivity Pr., 1995.

Bruce, Anne and Pepitone, James S. *Motivating Employees.* New York: Mcgraw-Hill, 1998.

Conklin, Robert. *How to Get People to Do Things.* Chicago: Contemporary Books, Inc. 1979.

Daniels, Aubrey, *Bringing Out the Best in People:How to Apply the Astonishing Power of Positive Reinforcement.* New York: McGraw-Hill, 1999.

Daniels, Dr. Aubrey C. *Bringing Out the Best in People.* New York: McGraw-Hill, Inc. 1994

Deeprose, Donna. *How to Recognize and Reward Employees.*
New York: AMACOM, 1994.

"Is Your Recognition Program Understood?," by Gillian Flynn, copyright
July 1998. Used with permission of ACC Communications/*Workforce*, Costa
Mesa, CA. Web site http://www.workforceonline.com. All rights reserved.

Herzberg, Frederick, Mausner, B., and Snyderman, B.B. *The Motivation to Work.*
New York: John Wiley & Sons. 1959.

Kinlaw, Dennis. *Coaching for Commitment.*
San Francisco: Jossey-Bass Pfeiffer, 1992.

Klubnik, Joan. *Rewarding and Recognizing Employees.*
New York: McGraw Hill, 1995.

Kreitner, Robert, and Kinicki, Angelo. *Organizational Behavior.*
Boston: Irwin/McGraw Hill, 1998.

Maslow, A. H., "A Theory of Human Motivation,"
Psychological Review, July 1943.

Murray, H. A. *Exploration in Personality.*
New York: John Wiley & Sons, 1938.

Nelson, Bob. "Rewarding and Recognizing Employees."
Chicago: Successories.

Nelson, Bob. *1001 Ways To Reward Employees.*
New York: Workman Publishing, 1994.

Skinner, Nancy. *Be Bright, Be Brief, Be Gone.*
Grand Rapids: Biggs/Gilmore Communications, 1992.

Weinstein, Matt. *Managing to Have Fun.*
New York: Simon & Schuster, 1996.

Weinstein, Matt. *Managing to Have Fun.*
New York: Simon & Schuster Inc. 1997.

Sources Cited

Dr. Aubrey C. Daniels. *Bringing Out The Best In People.*
New York: McGraw Hill, Inc., 1994, p 29.

"Is Your Recognition Program Understood?," by Gillian Flynn, copyright
July 1998. Used with permission of ACC Communications/*Workforce*,
Costa Mesa, CA. Web site http://www.workforceonline.com.
All rights reserved. p 32.

Joan P. Klubnik. *Rewarding and Recognizing Employees.*
New York: McGraw-Hill, 1995, p.9

"Are Your Staffers Happy? They're in the Minority,"
Supervisory Management, March 1996, p 11.

Chip R. Bell and Ron Zemke. *Managing Knock Your Socks Off Service.*
New York: AMACOM, 1992, pp 169, 184.

Kenneth Blanchard, and Spencer Johnson. *The One Minute Manager.*
New York: Berkley Books, 1981.

Bob Nelson. *Rewarding And Recognizing Employees.*
New York: McGraw-Hill, 1995, p.5

Robert Conklin. *How To Get People To Do Things.*
Chicago: Contemporary Books, 1979, p 3.

Janis Allen with Gail Snyder. *I Saw What You Did and I Know
Who You Are: Bloopers, Blunders and Success Stories on Giving
and Receiving Recognition.*
Tucker, GA: Performance Management Publications, 1990, p 106.

Dennis Kinlaw. *Coaching For Commitment.*
San Francisco: Jossey-Bass Pfeiffer, 1992, p 8.

Shopping List: Where To Buy Ingredients

Keep Recognition Tools at Your Fingertips,
Building Your Own Kit is Easy.

Baudville's exclusive portfolio of products were developed to fit a wide array of recognition needs. Simply select the products that work for you and your recognition team, choose a designer box to keep them organized and start celebrating recognition!

Please refer to Baudville's catalog for specific item details or visit us on the web. www.baudville.com. For personal assistance regarding inquiries and ordering information call: 1-800-728-0888

Joy of Recognition Kit

Joy of Recognition Kit

Includes *The Joy of Recognition* book, 50 Tell Us About You cards, 72 Coupons, Days of Praise Reminder, Formal Pocket Praise™, 6 pads of Recognition Post-It® Notes, 100 Sweet Sentiments Lollipops, 12 Celebration Assortment Greeting Cards and 5 Squeezable Praise Stars. Your Joy of Recognition Kit items will come packaged in a sturdy, reusable box so everything you need is at your fingertips. Ask for item #92743.

Joy of Recognition Deluxe Kit

This kit includes *Recognition FUNdamentals Software* and all items listed for the Joy of Recognition Kit.

The software includes certificate layouts, coupons, award titles, verses, clipart and a free paper sampler. Ask for item #12743.

Index

Index of Charts

Index of Recipes

Seasonal/Anniversary